CONSUMER CACOPHONY

ALSO AVAILABLE FROM BLOOMSBURY:

Prehistoric Philosophy, Justin Pack
Dump Philosophy, Michael Marder
Searching for the Anthropocene, Christopher Schaberg

CONSUMER CACOPHONY

The Catastrophe of Modern Abundance

JUSTIN PACK

BLOOMSBURY ACADEMIC
LONDON • NEW YORK • OXFORD • NEW DELHI • SYDNEY

BLOOMSBURY ACADEMIC

Bloomsbury Publishing Plc, 50 Bedford Square, London, WC1B 3DP, UK
Bloomsbury Publishing Inc, 1359 Broadway, New York, NY 10018, USA
Bloomsbury Publishing Ireland, 29 Earlsfort Terrace, Dublin 2, D02 AY28, Ireland

BLOOMSBURY, BLOOMSBURY ACADEMIC and the Diana logo are trademarks of Bloomsbury Publishing Plc

First published in Great Britain 2026

Copyright © Justin Pack, 2026

Justin Pack has asserted his right under the Copyright, Designs and Patents Act, 1988, to be identified as Author of this work.

Cover design: Ben Anslow
Cover images: *Christ In Limbo* (1575) by Hieronymus Bosch, Oil on wood (22 7/8 × 28 3/8 in | 58.1 × 72.1 cm) (© Public domain / Image provided by Indianapolis Museum of Art); Receipt (© wachiwit / AdobeStock)

All rights reserved. No part of this publication may be: i) reproduced or transmitted in any form, electronic or mechanical, including photocopying, recording or by means of any information storage or retrieval system without prior permission in writing from the publishers; or ii) used or reproduced in any way for the training, development or operation of artificial intelligence (AI) technologies, including generative AI technologies. The rights holders expressly reserve this publication from the text and data mining exception as per Article 4(3) of the Digital Single Market Directive (EU) 2019/790.

Bloomsbury Publishing Plc does not have any control over, or responsibility for, any third-party websites referred to or in this book. All internet addresses given in this book were correct at the time of going to press. The author and publisher regret any inconvenience caused if addresses have changed or sites have ceased to exist, but can accept no responsibility for any such changes.

A catalogue record for this book is available from the British Library.

A catalog record for this book is available from the Library of Congress.

ISBN: HB: 978-1-3505-0092-1
PB: 978-1-3505-0093-8
ePDF: 978-1-3505-0094-5
eBook: 978-1-3505-0095-2

Typeset by Deanta Global Publishing Services, Chennai, India
Printed and bound in Great Britain

For product safety related questions contact productsafety@bloomsbury.com.

To find out more about our authors and books visit www.bloomsbury.com and sign up for our newsletters.

CONTENTS

Introduction: The Problem of Too Much 1

1 Nietzsche's Instincts against Cacophony 15

2 Ortega y Gasset and the *Selva Selvaggia* 41

3 Hannah Arendt and *Amor Mundi* 63

4 The Dual Structure of Cacophonous Capitalism 89

5 Production and Transgression in Liquid Modernity 115

6 Social Media and Contemporary Changes 147

Conclusion 177

Bibliography 193

Index 198

Introduction
The Problem of Too Much

In what is arguably the culminating work of her illustrious career, Nancy Fraser claims in *Cannibal Capitalism*: "In this situation [the current global environmental crisis], safeguarding the planet requires building a counterhegemony. What is needed, in other words, is to resolve the present cacophony of opinion into an ecopolitical common sense that can orient a broadly shared project of transformation."[1] Fraser is specifically trying to get feminists, environmentalists, antiracists, critical theorists, and supporters of democracy on the same page and united in an anti-capitalism that brings together their diverse concerns. In seeking a "counterhegemony" she is rejecting the idea that the "system" can be fought piecemeal.

But overcoming cacophony is immensely difficult. Fraser's approach seeks to cut through the cacophony of the great variety of theoretical differences, opinions, and practices of these diverse radical movements by articulating how cannibal capitalism mutually endangers women, the environment, Black and Brown people, the poor, and democracy. In other words, she seeks to show that these groups are in the same boat and threatened by the same leviathan. If she can provide a sufficiently compelling rallying cry, perhaps they will pull together, put aside their differences, and fight the monster.

Critically, the leviathan of cannibal capitalism is itself overwhelmingly cacophonous. This is a problem Fraser does not address. While her account of capitalism as cannibalistic is compelling and invokes images of zombies or vampires, the cacophonous nature of modern consumer capitalism presents something much more protean, slippery, and incomprehensible: something like a Lovecraftian Cthulhu.

I think Fraser is right that we need to build a counterhegemony and that this involves overcoming cacophony. While I find her image of cannibal capitalism compelling, I want to look at the problem of cacophony itself, which she does not address. While she discusses the problem of cacophony at the level of radical movements, my primary focus is on the broader question of Cthulhu-like monstrosity of cacophonous capitalism. How do we deal with something so vast, incomprehensible, and alien? Worse, how do we hear each other or sound out idols when we are perpetually sonically blasted by the discordant babel of advertising sirens and petty influencers? Let me introduce what I mean by this.

The problem of cacophony refers to sound—the tumult of excessive and overwhelming noise. But consumer cacophony assaults all the physical senses as well as our mental capacities. Broadly, it is the problem of too much:

> There is just too much. Too much to think about, too much to hold on to, too much to fight against. Too many people to talk to, too many restaurants to eat at, and definitely, definitely too many movies to watch ... We asked ourselves, why add to the noise?[2]

Suppose the most meaningful, important, wonderful philosophy text ever is written or discovered. Would it make it to press? What if it was written by a nonacademic? What if it was written by a non-tenure track lecturer working at a community college? What if it was written by an eighth-century Tang dynasty scholar or a Mexican Jesuit priest in the 1600s?

If it made it to press, would people read it? Would they understand and appreciate it? Probably not. We have so many great works of art, literature, and philosophy that we couldn't read them in a lifetime. We have so many mediocre works that it is hard to know sometimes which are great works. We have so many bad works that most everyone doomscrolls instead.

In the film *Se7en*, John Doe orchestrates horrific and hypersensational crimes that embody the seven deadly sins. He hopes the extremity of these terrible scenes will shock people out of their moral lethargy and wake them up to contemporary evils: "Wanting people to listen, you can't just tap them on the shoulder anymore. You have to hit them with a sledgehammer. And then you'll notice you've got their strict attention." The cynical young detective responds condescendingly: "All this work, two months from now, no one's gonna care, no one's gonna give a shit, no one's gonna remember."[3]

This is the same plight faced by modern advertising and modern media. How to draw attention to yet another product in a sea of commercial goods? How to cut through the noise and get the clicks? We currently live in what Thomas Hylland Eriksen calls the "tyranny of the moment."[4] We are inundated with news, ads, tweets, information, offers, demands, stories, and so on. Trends come and go quickly, attention is ever-shifting to the newest gadget, the latest scandal—how, in this cacophony, is anyone going to see and hear, much less pay attention to our hypothetical most important philosophy text ever?

Will it not, like most other things, just be lost in the noise? The social theorist Zygmunt Bauman summarizes this conundrum: "A specter hovers over the denizens of the liquid-modern world and all their labors and creations: the specter of superfluity."[5]

We have reached an odd position—one that Hans Jonas called "the threat of catastrophe from excessive success."[6] It is clear that our technological and economic successes are having terrible environmental consequences. But the concerns I am raising here also concern fundamental questions of meaning and morality for humans. We have created a cacophony and now must ask, how, in a society inundated with too much, we can establish and/or preserve coherent shared meanings and institutions? Can democracy function in a society drowning in advertising, twenty-four-hour news and media? How are we to competently take responsibility for political and social issues when we are busy choosing between Coke or Pepsi?

This is a radical change in the quality of the world around us. As Charles Taylor points out, we can see it in our cities:

> Contrast a medieval city crowded around its Gothic cathedral with a modern metropolis. It's not just that skyscrapers now dwarf the cathedral, if one remains. This might be seen as reflecting a new set of meanings which have taken over the old, say Capitalism replacing Christianity. But actually, the change is more drastic. It is more like cacophony replacing meaning as such. The shape of the city no longer manifests a single over-arching meaning, but on the one hand, individual great buildings each monumentalize some corporation or triumphant entrepreneur, while on the other, vast areas of city form a crazy quilt of special purpose constructions—

factories, malls, docks—following each some fragmented instrumental rationality . . .

On another level, the 'atonal banshee of emerging egomania' unavoidably impinges through the ubiquity of advertising and the entertainment media, insistently calling us each to our own satisfaction and fulfillment, linking the powerful forces of sexual desire and the craving for wholeness, constitutive elements of our humanity, to products promoted to the status of icons, and in the process obscuring, emptying, and trivializing these forces themselves.[7]

In this remarkable description, Taylor claims we are not seeing "Capitalism replacing Christianity" but "cacophony replacing meaning." I want to suggest what we are seeing is both: we can simultaneously have an overwhelming, cacophonous tumult with a central orienting logic, the logic of accumulation. The latter drives the former. It functions like a constant that both drives but suffuses the explosion of meanings and possibilities that Taylor calls the "nova effect."

The dual structure of the cacophonous nova effect will be critical to this analysis. The stable core of the nova effect is not just a central orienting logic of accumulation—in fact, multiple commenters have claimed the logic of accumulation should be seen as one part of a new religion or moral order with a new spirituality that includes a moral image of the ideal human, *homo economicus*, a disciplined calculative rationality, and a politics of meritocracy that sanctifies accumulation.[8] This moral order creates a world of money: abstract money people, calculative, and quantitative money thought, accumulation-driven money dreams. But it is a kind of subtle and insidious religion that has no need to proselytize since it can quietly colonize entire lifeworlds, infiltrating, and mingling with traditional beliefs like an all-pervading parasite, tolerating, preserving, and profiting off anything that doesn't fundamentally reject the core logic of accumulation. While the indefatigable logic of accumulation drives the cacophonous nova effect, the stable core constellation of moral, personal, and social ideals centered on meritocratic work and money can always be invoked as the wizard behind the curtain, the eye of the storm, the invisible hand, the rationality in what may look like chaos.

Since this dual structure seems to hold two opposites together, it can be difficult to grasp. It means that the same city/culture/society could be experienced by one person as oppressively noisy, disorienting, and chaotic, while another could find the same place oppressively simple, totalitarian, and vulgar in its fundamental, all-encompassing logic of accumulation. One might find a world full of different confusing life choices and meaning-bestowing narratives; another might find a subtle, new religion of spiritualized accumulation that comfortingly undergirds the noise. Thus, while I will be discussing the cacophonous nova effect as a moral and social danger, many do not experience it this way. For many, this proliferating nova effect seems liberating:

> This new setting opens unprecedented vistas. Freedom of self-creation has never before achieved a similarly breathtaking scope—simultaneously exciting and frightening. Never before was the need for orientation points and guidance as strong and as painfully felt. Yet never before were firm and reliable orientation points and trustworthy guides in such short supply.... That shortage coincides with a proliferation of tempting suggestions and seductive offers of

orientation and with a rising wave of guidebooks amid swelling throngs of counselors.[9]

While we have a subtle but ubiquitous calling to be a good *homo economicus*, make money, accumulate, and be productive, we must also choose paths in life, purposes that provide opportunities for how we want to spend our free time and money.[10] We have the freedom and curse to ostensibly make and remake ourselves into who we want to be, a DIY life: "who are you?" amounts to "what do you do?" and "what do you do for fun?" that is, what is your career and what brings you joy/gives you meaning? Over the course of a life, we may cycle through many different, overlapping, and simultaneous meaningful "purposes." Such meaning-giving purposes become individualized, and as we shift from one activity to the next, we join and immerse ourselves to different degrees in the vast diversity of resulting "neo-tribes" of meaning (some examples: fans of the Great British Baking show, fans of the New York Yankees, alumni of USC, patriotic Germans, Zen Buddhists, Android users, members of PETA, etc.).[11]

But, as Zygmunt Bauman indicates above, this freedom of self-creation hides a nihilistic underside. Each of these new possibilities and opportunities, by virtue of their explosive and accelerating number, are mutually fragile, and ultimately, if we have chosen them, we know in the back of our minds that we could abandon them whenever we find the next shiny thing.[12] As a result, the hold of these life projects/purposes tends to be tenuous.

Some thinkers find this a positive development that allows for diversity and encourages tolerance.[13] Others worry the result of the broiling cacophony described by Taylor is often an odd and awkward nihilism that can result in exhaustion from the endless titillation and excitation and can become comfortable and miserable. Cast adrift in cacophonous seas, many escape or settle into transience:

> Question: If someone from the 1950s suddenly appeared today, what would be the most difficult thing to explain to them about life today?
>
> Answer: I possess a device, in my pocket, that is capable of accessing the entirety of information known to humanity. I use it to look at pictures of cats and get in arguments with strangers.[14]

We love to tell ourselves life is better than ever before. GDP is up, life expectancy is up, we have more freedoms than ever. The latest, most exciting Netflix series releases next month. But it is not clear that, for all our wonderful technologies and advancements, we have created a meaningful existence that encourages human flourishing. It may be, as Nietzsche worried, that we have created a nihilistic abundance:

> What I combat is economic optimism: as if increasing expenditure of everybody must necessarily involve the increasing welfare of everybody. The opposite seems to me to be the case: expenditure of everybody amounts to a collective loss: man is diminished—so one no longer knows what aim this tremendous process has served.[15]

It may be, as Osage Big Chief claimed, that

> I see and admire your manner of living, your good warm houses, your extensive fields of corn, your gardens, your cows, oxen, workhouses, wagons, and a thousand machines that I know not the use of. I see that are able to clothe yourselves, even from

weeds and grass. In short, you even do almost what you choose. You whites possess the power of subduing almost every animal to your use. You are surrounded by slaves. Everything about you is in chains, and you are slaves yourselves. I fear if I should exchange my pursuits for yours, I too should become a slave.[16]

This book seeks to examine modern cacophony as a nihilistic abundance that threatens a "catastrophe from excessive success." This abundance has proven to be a critical threat to the world in two senses. First, to the physical world: the environment and the planet we live on. But, second, it has also proven a critical threat to our spiritual and cultural worlds, compromising their coherence.

The problem of too much has historically concerned many thinkers.[17] Unfortunately, considering the compounding nature of the problem of too much, recent philosophers have struggled to confront it seriously. If anything, they are complicit in it. In part, this is due to the neoliberalization of academia and the increasing demands of academic productivity. I have written about this elsewhere.[18] Here I want to examine another contributing factor. I will claim this failure is largely because the totalitarian logic of accumulation does not fit with the typical understanding of what constitutes a totalitarian threat. Normally this is taken to be something like an overwhelming force that seeks to trap, limit, and control us, like an Orwellian government or avaricious factory owners. And resisting oppressive control seems to require breaking out of fetters, seeking freedom, transgressing, and challenging authority. But the cacophonous logic of nihilistic abundance embraces transgression and ostensibly provides us with more freedoms and possibilities, as long as we play the accumulation game—or at least don't resist it. Breaking out, seeking new possibilities and freedoms, celebrating difference—these are all potentially commodifiable and profitable enterprises. Cacophonous capitalism welcomes such efforts, invites all to the party, and overwhelms with its dazzling abundance.

This anti-totalizing logic of transgression and diffusion is understandably common in radical movements, but they are often in danger of feeding the beast they are fighting against. Fraser has argued this is the case of feminism. She claims that feminist efforts to push back against the constraints of the welfare state capitalism's nuclear family were appropriated by later neoliberal capitalism:

> Our critique of the family wage supplies a good part of the romance that invests flexible capitalism with a higher meaning and a moral point. Endowing their daily struggles with an ethical meaning, the feminist romance attracts women at both ends of the social spectrum: at one end, the female cadres off the professional middle classes, determined to crack the glass ceiling; at the other end, the female temps, part-timers, low-wage service workers and microcredit borrowers, seeking not only income and material security, but also dignity, self-betterment and liberation from traditional authority. At both ends, the dream of women's emancipation is harnessed to the engine of capitalist accumulation. Thus, second-wave feminism's critique of the family wage has enjoyed a perverse afterlife.[19]

Variations on this conundrum have played out in other radical movements: efforts to transgress or outrun cacophonous capitalism are often reappropriated by it. This is precisely why Fraser seeks to overcome the cacophony of radical movements with a counterhegemony, not a diffusive approach.

The idea of seeking a "counterhegemony" is one that goes contrary to much of the anti-totalitarian "postmodern" sentiment. But if you go back 100 years, you find figures that clearly recognized the need for "counterhegemony." Perhaps the most obvious is Nietzsche, who presciently rejected both the nihilism of cacophony and the nihilism of the logic of accumulation—challenging directly the dual structure of cacophonous capitalism. As such, Nietzsche will be a particularly important figure in my analysis. But Nietzsche also hoped for a "revaluation of values," a counterhegemony to help found a healthier world. Other thinkers, like Ortega y Gasset and Hannah Arendt, for example, also saw the importance of resisting cacophony and seeking counterhegemony. Ortega y Gasset wrestled with these issues in the context of the onslaught of new ideas and practices in modernizing Spain. Arendt worried about how cacophonous capitalism consumes worlds and empties them of strength.

In what follows, I want to turn first to each of these three thinkers who rightfully worried about the consumer age they saw unfolding before them. Each questions the danger of cacophony in important ways and will help articulate a fuller understanding of it.

With these critiques established, Chapter 4 will examine the dual structure of cacophonous capitalism more fully.

Then, in Chapter 5, I will use the thought of Zygmunt Bauman to trace an example of the logic of postmodern, anti-totalizing, transgressive radical movements. Bauman's shift from the language of "postmodern" to "liquid modern" over the course of his writings will help illustrate the tensions that can lead to cacophony in radical movements instead of counterhegemony.

In Chapter 6, I address the cacophonous effects of social media and the internet in general.

Finally, in Chapter 7, I will return to Fraser and the task of counterhegemony. If there is too much, might it be correct to stop?

Notes

1 Fraser, Nancy. *Cannibal Capitalism: How Our System is Devouring Democracy, Care and the Planet—and What We Can Do about It* (New York, NY: Verso, 2022), 77.

2 https://a24films.com/notes/2022/04/miracle-work-a-note-from-daniels, accessed December 27, 2022.

3 Se7en, David Fincher, 1995.

4 Eriksen, Thomas Hylland. *The Tyranny of the Moment: Fast and Slow Time in the Information Age* (Las Vegas, NV: Pluto Press, 2001).

5 Bauman, Zygmunt. *Does Ethics Stand a Chance in a World of Consumers?* (Cambridge, MA: Harvard University Press, 2008), 185.

6 Jonas, Hans. *The Imperative of Responsibility: In Search of an Ethics of a Technological Age* (Chicago, IL: University of Chicago Press, 1985), 140.

7 Taylor, Charles. *A Secular Age* (Cambridge, MA: Harvard University Press, 2007), 552.

8 This has been argued by more than one author: Cox, Harvey. *The Market as God* (Cambridge, MA: Harvard University Press, 2016), Boldeman, Lee. *The Cult of the Market: Economic Fundamentalism and its Discontents* (Canberra, Australia: ANU E Press, 2011), McCarraher, Eugene. *The Enchantments of Mammon: How Capitalism became the Religion of Modernity* (Cambridge, MA: Belknap Press of Harvard University Press, 2019).

9 Bauman, Zygmunt. *Does Ethics Stand a Chance in a World of Consumers?* (Cambridge, MA: Harvard University Press, 2008), 24–5.

10 The fact that we speak of "spending" time as if it were cash, indicates how deeply capitalistic thinking has infiltrated our everyday language.
11 Bauman calls these "neo-tribes." *Thinking Sociologically* (Cambridge, MA: Blackwell Publishers, 1990).
12 Young, Julian. *The Death of God and the Meaning of Life* (New York, NY: Routledge, 2014).
13 Giddens, Anthony. *The Consequences of Modernity* (Stanford: Stanford University Press, 1991).
14 https://www.reddit.com/r/AskReddit/comments/15yaap/if_someone_from_the_1950s_suddenly_appeared_today/. Accessed July 5, 2019.
15 Nietzsche, Friedrich. *The Will to Power* (New York, NY: Vintage, 1968), 866.
16 Quoted in Deloria, Jr., Vine. *Spirit and Reason: The Vine Deloria, Jr., Reader* (Golden, CO: Fulcrum, 1999), 4.
17 Blair, Ann M. *Too Much to Know: Managing Scholarly Information before the Modern Age* (New Haven, CT: Yale University Press, 2011).
18 Pack, Justin. *How the Neoliberalization of Academia Leads to Thoughtlessness: Arendt and the Modern University* (New York: Lexington Books, 2018).
19 Fraser, Nancy. "Feminism, Capitalism, and the Cunning of History." *New Left Review*, 56 (Mar/Apr 2009): 110–11.

1
Nietzsche's Instincts against Cacophony

The problem of too much is not a new one. As Ann Blair has shown, concerns about managing too much existed long before modernity.[1] But the philosophical concern with the problem of too much has waxed and waned historically, drawing the attention of some thinkers while not appearing in others. With the rise of consumer society, the problem of too much begins to take a more prominent role in some philosophers like Kierkegaard, Schopenhauer, Nietzsche, Ortega y Gasset, Arendt, and Hans Jonas. But, oddly, as this problem has become exponentially exacerbated in the last fifty years—especially with the internet and social media—there has not been a proportional corresponding increase in serious philosophical analysis of it (with a few exceptions like the work of Zygmunt Bauman, Han Byung-Chul, etc.).

This book attempts to place this problem front and center by analyzing the problem of too much as the problem of cacophony. The word "cacophony" suggests overwhelming, dissonant noise that makes it hard to concentrate and think. It represents, then, something that contributes greatly to the pervasive thoughtlessness we see in modern life.[2]

What exactly is cacophony? Why is it a threat? And why, if it is such a problem, does it seem to receive so little contemporary philosophical attention? It is precisely due to the lack of contemporary philosophical attention that to begin to understand the threat of cacophony, I will turn to three thinkers that wrestled with these issues in the context of the rise of consumer society: Nietzsche, Ortega y Gasset, and Arendt. With this background in place, I will theorize the dual structure of contemporary cacophony. I have offered an initial outline of this structure in the introduction, but the dynamics involved will become increasingly clear as we assess the threat of cacophony according to these thinkers. Nietzsche is a particularly important thinker for understanding and introducing this structure because he condemns both the logic of accumulation that is at the heart of and drives the cacophonous nova effect and the resulting cacophony itself. Both are nihilistic according to Nietzsche.

Once we have examined the threat of cacophony and its contemporary structure, we can examine why it hasn't garnered more attention from contemporary thinkers and what are the ethical implications of production in a cacophonous society.

Let's begin with Nietzsche.

Nietzsche: Historical Context and Influences

Amid the philosophizing with a hammer, the attack upon Christianity and the declaration that God is dead, it can be difficult to remember that Nietzsche begins, in many ways, as a romantic conservative. His early works show a clear concern for community and place that inform his critique of cacophony. As Julian Young has argued, Nietzsche's initial romantic concerns with (authentic) community may remain even in his later works.³ This chapter attempts to show that if we take these positions of early Nietzsche seriously, he emerges as an important, if perhaps surprising, thinker of place and community and an intense critic of modern cacophony. Central to understanding this critique is Nietzsche's concept of "instincts" and how they relate to nihilism. Nietzsche claims that the logic of accumulation is a terrible, nihilistic set of instincts, while the cacophony of lifeways represents a confusion and loss of instincts. Since good instincts are the key to a full, non-nihilist life, both the core and nova effect of cacophony result in nihilism.

Nietzsche wrote at a time when the radical disruption of society as a result of the Industrial Revolution was becoming more apparent on the continent.⁴ Both Germany (Prussia) and Italy had begun a rapid process of attempting to gather together medieval city-states and princedoms into modern nations. This resulted in the sundering of traditional communities, their standardization or homogenization into new modern societies, and the cacophonous proliferations of capitalism. It is not surprising that one of the major questions of the nineteenth century concerned the question of community and meaning in the increasingly fast, complex, sprawling modern world.

Nietzsche's romantic conservatism is apparent in his early lectures *On the Future of Our Educational Institutions* delivered in 1872. In these seldom read and often forgotten lectures, Nietzsche reacts to the modernization of Germany. His primary concern is that the expansion and democratization of education are weakening and undermining it.[5] This is, in turn, an expression of a larger problem:

> This expansion belongs to the most beloved of the dogmas of modern political economy. As much knowledge and education as possible; therefore the greatest possible supply and demand—hence as much happiness as possible:—that is the formula. In this case utility is made the object and goal of education,—utility in the sense of gain—the greatest possible pecuniary gain.[6]

For Nietzsche, this is a betrayal of "Goethe, Schiller, Lessing, and Winckelmann" and the vision of the Greeks as the "real home of culture."[7] It is the replacement of the dream of a noble culture with one focused on the production of the "money earning creature."[8]

Here Nietzsche shows both his conservative and his romantic colors. Politically he is interested in neither democracy nor liberalism. These, he thinks, have resulted in a mediocre, money-obsessed machine society. But Nietzsche objects not only to the results of liberalism and democracy; he also rejects the assumptions about reason and human nature that founded them. Like the Romantics, Nietzsche finds the glorification of reason to be superficially inattentive to the complicated depths of what it is to be human.[9] Also like the Romantics, he thinks the atomistic individualism of liberalism completely fails to do justice to the necessity of human community.[10]

Enlightenment thinkers tended to stress a narrative of progress—the forward march of civilization and science, the fading away of superstition.[11] Romantics, especially German Romantics, tended to reverse the progress narrative and instead proposed that there was occurring a fall from grace. According to this narrative, the height of civilization occurred in Greece, and Western society has never since returned to those heights.¹² Against the Enlightenment, Romantics stressed the importance of myth, the loss of community in modernity, and even the importance of religion. Myth, community, and religion were often seen as being interrelated.¹³

The romantic concern with community and myth is clear in *The Birth of Tragedy*. Perhaps surprisingly for many readers of Nietzsche, Julian Young has argued, rightly I think, that if we keep these things in mind we can describe Nietzsche as having a philosophy of religion.¹⁴ This could be alternatively formulated as a philosophy of community. Clearly, it is with these particular concerns in the forefront that Nietzsche first develops his critique of cacophony.

It is important to recognize and hold strongly onto this background because after Nietzsche breaks with Wagner, he seems to drop the language of myth and community and increasingly uses a language that seems to privilege the individual as the source of the fight against nihilism. Thus, we get the language of overcoming, "preparatory human beings,"¹⁵ "faith in oneself,"¹⁶ the "supra-national nomadic type of man,"¹⁷ of the Übermensch, and so on. Very influential interpretations of Nietzsche, like Walter Kaufmann's *Nietzsche: Philosopher, Psychologist, Antichrist* and Alexander Nehemas' *Nietzsche: Life as Literature* have led to the common view in Anglophone interpretation that Nietzsche is an individualist.¹⁸

But Young argues that this is a mistake. Attention to the ways in which Nietzsche's early focus on myth and instincts continues to inform both his later criticisms of cacophony and makes it difficult to take seriously that Nietzsche simply abandons his early vision and adopts a kind of individualism (especially after Nietzsche radically challenges the Cartesian self). Young's argument is that, properly understood, Nietzsche's call for "higher types" is not just a call for a higher type to reject modernity, but to find new instincts that help overcome the nihilistic cacophony.[19] I will make a more modest claim that even if we do accept that the language of community and myth recedes after Nietzsche's break with Wagner, the language of instincts, which appears with community and myth in the early works, most clearly does not recede in the later works—if anything, it becomes stronger. At the very least, this means that the standard Anglophone individualist interpretation needs to account for how instincts, which are both clearly social and a key part of Nietzsche's critique of cacophonous modernity, fit with this individualism. Kaufmann doesn't even give "instincts" a unique entry in the index of *The Will to Power* and instead directs the reader to see "passion(s)."[20] It is worth noting that a conference centered on Young's claims was held in 2012 and the book *Individual and Community in Nietzsche's Philosophy* was published three years later with ten papers on the topic.[21] I could not find any discussion of instincts in any of the papers, nor is it included in the index.

I will attempt to rectify this omission by arguing that any attempt to understand Nietzsche's critique of cacophonous modernity must take instincts into account. I will argue that instincts are the deeply embedded social understandings humans gain (indeed, are born into) through myth, that is, the narratives that establish a tradition that unites and gives direction to a particular people. Nietzsche thinks there are healthy instincts and unhealthy instincts and characterizes modernity as creating societies with, on the one hand, a core of unhealthy accumulative instincts combined with, on the other, a cacophonous disarray of instincts. These might seem like contradictory states of instincts at first, but they are actually interrelated and feed off each other. To make this claim clear, I first need to show how instincts are related to myth and human flourishing. To do so, I turn now to *The Birth of Tragedy*.

The Birth of Tragedy: The Affirmation of Life

Throughout Nietzsche's writings, one of his primary concerns is the affirmation of life. At the most basic level, Nietzsche's critique of cacophonous modernity is that it does not result in the affirmation of life. To understand why it does not require understanding what he thinks does result in the affirmation of life. This is first outlined in *The Birth of Tragedy*.

At this early point in his writings, Nietzsche is still in some ways a follower of Schopenhauer. Like his teacher, Nietzsche thinks that life is full of pain and suffering. Nietzsche relates a Greek story in which "the wise Silenius" says the most desirable thing is to not be born or—failing that—to die.[22] Nietzsche thinks the Greeks were honest in this estimation and knew something was needed to redeem life. The solution is art:

> Art approaches, as a redeeming and healing enchantress; she alone may transform these horrible reflections on the terror and absurdity of existence into representations with which man may live. These are the representation of the sublime as the artistic conquest of the awful, and of the comic as the artistic release from the nausea of the absurd.[23]

Somehow then, art can offer us "metaphysical comfort."[24] Nietzsche thinks Greek tragedy is especially good at seducing us into believing "that, in spite of the flux of phenomena, life at bottom is indestructibly powerful and pleasurable . . ."[25] How is this done?

Nietzsche describes two interconnected and somewhat opposed drives, the Apollonian and the Dionysian, which he thinks combine in Greek tragedy to justify existence.[26] The Apollonian, according to Nietzsche, corresponds to the art of sculpture, dreams, and individuation.[27] This is because their namesake, Apollo, is the god of perfection "in contrast to the incompletely intelligible everyday world."[28] Greek sculptures portray perfectly muscled figures, dreams focus on only the necessary and intelligible, and individuation creates the (artificial) distances necessary to make useful distinctions and simplifications. The Apollonian therefore creates a perfected, glorified illusion of reality that is more beautiful and more attractive than mundane, painful reality.

The Dionysian, on the other hand, corresponds to music, drunkenness, pain, and dissolution. Dionysian festivals are orgiastic, violent revelries that destroy life and dissolve individuality.[29] More positively, the Dionysian is a kind of ecstasy which can unify the self with others (or dissolve the self in others), with nature, or with some greater whole, and in so doing has a transformative power.[30]

There are limitations to the Dionysian and the Apollonian drives.[31] Nietzsche sees imperial Rome as the Apollonian drive for glory gone mad—untempered by the Dionysian. He sees India as the Dionysian pessimism and "indifference" mired in mysticism without the uplifting Apollonian.[32] Only the Greeks (conveniently geographically located between them) learned the proper balance that allows for the highest flourishing of humanity. This was achieved in Greek tragedy.

The basic human problem, for Nietzsche, is pain. The genius of Greek tragedy was to induce (Dionysian) pain in the audience and then make it meaningful through (Apollonian) glorification. The pain then appears as a necessary part of a glorious life. Importantly, for Nietzsche, the Greeks did not avoid or eliminate pain, as we moderns attempt to do, but found a way to affirm it as an important part of a meaningful life. In so doing, Greek tragedy taught how to live in a way that affirmed life—all of life—including the ugly and painful parts.

Greek tragedy was, of course, a communal experience. The audience, through the chorus, which represented the wisdom and traditions of the city or community, was swallowed into the play—sucked into and immersed in the story—such that the pain of the tragedy is their own pain and the glorious actions their own actions.[33] Through this Dionysian dissolution, the tragedy has a transformative or cathartic power over the community. It teaches and shapes on a level deeper than any formal training could hope to. It establishes instincts. The tragic play, like music, establishes a "myth."[34]

In *The Birth of Tragedy*, myth is "the concentrated picture of the world . . . abbreviature of phenomena."[35] The world is a very complicated place and there are many ways of making it intelligible. Myth simplifies the world and establishes a tradition for a particular people. Nietzsche says that "without myth, however, every culture loses its healthy creative natural power: it is only a horizon encompassed by myths that rounds off to unity a social movement."[36] Homer and the Greek tragedies were myths for Greeks. As we have seen, they are stories that glorify, unify, and give purpose to a people. They simplify the complicated world and bestow people with instincts that hopefully allow them to flourish.

Different traditions or communities have different myths and different instincts. Nietzsche characterizes Christianity as one such tradition that established a certain myth or set of myths as expounded in the Bible, in the stained-glass windows of Cathedrals, in stories of particular saints, in communal practices, etc. These myths expound a certain view of the world, of the self, of how one should act, of the nature of time, etc.—all these become embodied as instincts, the taken-for-granted ways of being and understandings that guide a community. Despite his many reservations about Christianity, Nietzsche recognizes that it made evil meaningful, gave life a certain purpose, and fended off nihilism for a period of time.[37] Every human community or tradition has a guiding set of myths which helps to organize a set of instincts—thus we speak of the Confucian tradition, the Buddhist tradition, the Islamic tradition, and so on—each with many variations. Not all of them do it as well as others, and Nietzsche thinks the Greeks did it the best.

The establishment of a healthy myth and healthy instincts that allow for the affirmation of life is Nietzsche's goal. Whatever we make of the history here, Nietzsche is painting, in ancient Greece, a picture of how to affirm life—a dream he hoped Wagner was bringing forth in Germany.[38] Nietzsche wanted "the rebirth of German myth."[39] He also wanted healthy instincts. In the next section, I examine what he means by this.

Instincts

The word "instincts" is a key word throughout Nietzsche's writings. The connotations of animality, physicality, and non-rationality are all implied in Nietzsche's use of the term. It is clearly meant as an overturning of some of the basic Western ideas of what it means to be human. One may see this by contrasting Nietzsche with the Cartesian position. After doubting every kind of object, Descartes discovers "I think therefore I am"—to be human is to be a thinking thing.[40] To be human is to have and develop rationality. Rationality is what allows humans to understand the universe. But Nietzsche turns Descartes on his head and argues that thinking, rationality, and knowledge are NOT a solution or a key to a solution, but rather a problem: "Knowledge kills action, action requires the veil of illusion—it is the lesson Hamlet teaches . . . too much reflection, from a surplus of possibilities, never arrive at action at all."[41] This is an important point that is worth dwelling on. Nietzsche is pointing out that normal human action requires not reflecting. If we know how to drive a car, we don't have to think about it while we do it. In fact, if we are thinking about it, we are more likely to make a mistake. Thus, a comment commonly heard in sports: "she is thinking too much." Descartes, however, defines the human as essentially a thinking being. In so doing, he follows and pushes forward the Socratic dream of the rational human in a rational universe. Nietzsche thinks that this Socratic dream of the rational human discovering the laws of the universe is a terrible mistake. It is driven by "the profound illusion" which "consists in the imperturbable belief that, with the clue of logic, thinking can reach to the innermost depths of being, and that thinking can not only perceive being but even modify it."[42]

Nietzsche doesn't think either the world is as fathomable as Socrates wants it to be or the self is as rational as Descartes would like to think. He rejects Descartes description of thoughts being carefully examined and accepted or rejected by the spectator philosopher: "a thought comes when 'it' wishes, not when 'I' wish, so that it is a falsification of the facts of the case to say that the subject 'I' is the condition of the predicate 'think.' *It* thinks . . . ."[43] Contrary to Cartesian thought, the self is not like a computer that accesses data on demand.

Even stranger, often human beings experience the sensation of being torn within themselves and arguing with themselves. It is as if two different aspects of the self, or even multiple different selves, are arguing: "perhaps it is just as permissible to assume a multiplicity of subjects, whose interaction and struggle is the basis of our thought and our consciousness in general?"[44] At one point Nietzsche calls this multiplicity the "manifold thing" and argues that "our body is a social structure composed of many souls."[45] But he also speaks of "drives" working on a deeper level than consciousness.[46] These different drives can compete with each other, and what one conceives as oneself can suddenly seem like multiple selves debating, arguing, and fighting.

This manifold "thing" called the self is never as transparent as it seems. The reason we call it the "self" in the first place is to establish a sense of control.[47] This suggests that there is one dominant drive, some "I," that organizes the different strands that make up the self. Nietzsche's phenomenological description of the self makes it clear, however, that much of the self is hidden from the supposedly transparent self. Indeed, someone who trains herself to listen to these different impulses might be surprised at how little of herself she knows.

Nietzsche's analysis of the self as a manifold "thing" or a multiplicity may be extended to the world. Nietzsche thinks no amount of thinking about the manifold self or the world we live in could reduce either to an accurate and completely transparent representation. In

The Will to Power, he describes the world as "a monster of energy . . . a sea of forces flowing and rushing together, eternally changing, eternally flooding back . . ."[48] Although we cannot make the universe transparent, it is, however, imperative that human society have some way of navigating through the ever-shifting abundance lest it gets lost, and this is what myth allows. Myth carves a particular trajectory through the flux, provides a "concentrated picture" that hopefully will allow for healthy instincts and the affirmation of life. History is full of different traditions that have carved out a temporary home in the flux of reality, with varying degrees of success in terms of the health of their instincts. Nietzsche thinks the Greeks did it the best, but each creates a kind of sanctuary in the storm. Because myth is like the eye of a storm, the breakdown of "the mythical maternal home, the mythical maternal bosom" threatens to leave humanity adrift.[49]

All traditions tend to break down and disintegrate over time, but unfortunately for us, Nietzsche thinks we are reaching the culmination of a project, first outlined by Socrates, which aims to find something *eternally* solid amid the roiling, ever-shifting flood, something that would overcome the need for myths by finding solid ground. But despite its opposition to tradition and myth, which it characterizes as superstition, even this Socratic dream of making the universe transparent is itself a kind of myth. It offers its own way of navigating through the flux, its own instincts: "most of the conscious thinking of a philosopher is secretly guided and forced into certain channels by his instincts."[50] This is why Nietzsche calls Socrates, who he takes to be the father of this approach to life, "the mystagogue of science."[51] The problem is not only that Socrates and science don't recognize that they too are providing a new myth and new instincts, but,

Nietzsche thinks, that they give us life-denying instincts: "Whereas in all productive men it is instinct that is the creatively affirmative force, and consciousness that acts critically and dissuasively; with Socrates it is instinct that becomes critic, and consciousness that becomes creator—a perfect monstrosity *per defectum*!"[52] The modern instinct is to destroy all instincts, but instincts are the foundation of action.[53] Thus, in *Twilight of the Idols* Nietzsche concludes: "to have to fight the instincts—that is the formula for decadence: as long as life is ascending, happiness equals instinct."[54] When this anti-instinct instinct becomes widespread throughout a society, this results in nihilism. In modernity, this exacerbates cacophony.

The Critique of Modern Cacophony

As we have just seen, Nietzsche thinks we are seeing the final results of a massive project, initiated by Socrates but culminating in our own time, to make the world transparent, transform it, and therefore justify existence. This project claims to offer reason and truth to overcome tradition and superstition. It has spread, and continues to spread across the world, breaking apart traditional communities and replacing them with a bureaucratic, money-driven mass society. It unwittingly leads to a life-denying nihilism.

The modern project, the culmination of Socratism, fails to produce affirmation of life because it has an inadequate answer to the problem of pain. Greek tragedy succeeded by finding a way to make pain meaningful. The modern response is to attempt to eliminate or minimize pain. This establishes a new set of utilitarian instincts that

Nietzsche thinks are a terrible mistake: "But what if pleasure and displeasure were so tied together that whoever wanted to have as much possible one must also have as much as possible of the other—that whoever wanted to learn to 'jubilate up to the heavens' would also have to be prepared for 'depression until death'?"[55] The attempt to eliminate or minimize pain amounts to the diminution of the human capacity to feel, indeed, to be. With no "highs" of pain, there can be no "highs" of pleasure. The process of maximizing pleasure and minimizing pain, therefore, leads to a mediocre life of petty pleasures, "comfort and fashion."[56]

This utilitarian attempt to eliminate pain and increase pleasure has contributed to the creation of a money-driven society, as we saw in Nietzsche's earliest concerns. He remains highly critical of this throughout his works: "The most industrious of ages–ours–does not know to make anything of all its industriousness and money, except always still more money and still more industriousness."[57] The desperate effort to accumulate, combined with the need to maximize small pleasures, leads to the absurd situation in which "living in a constant chase after gain compels people to expend their spirit to the point of exhaustion in continual pretense and overreaching and anticipating others."[58] Pain is an inevitable part of human existence, and although modern consumer society promises its alleviation and offers myriad distractions and entertainments and pain killers, in the end, it cannot eliminate it. Because it does not find a way to make pain meaningful, as Greek tragedy did, it fails to deliver on its lofty promises.

All the modern industriousness produces ever more stuff but gives little direction beyond "avoid pain," "have fun," and accumulate. I take this to mean that despite the great means created in modernity, there is no consistent direction as to what to do with these means—there is not a healthy myth to provide some order to modern instincts. Like Socrates, modern humanity is left with "wantonness and anarchy of . . . instincts."[59] The result is a kind of cacophonous abundance that takes place in a vacuum:

> How could we drink up the sea? Who gave us the sponge to wipe away the entire horizon? What were we doing when we unchained this earth from its sun? Whither is it moving now? Whither are we moving? Away from all suns? Are we not plunging continually? Backwards, sideward, forward, in all directions? Is there still any up or down?[60]

Without the sun, without any suns, there is no longer any direction. "Men unlearn spontaneous action, they merely react to stimuli from outside."[61] Without any "sure instinct"[62] this noisy, cacophonous modernity is exhausting:

> For this is how things stand: the withering and leveling of European man constitutes *our* greatest danger, because it is a wearying sight. . . . Today we see nothing with any desire to be greater, we sense that everything is going increasingly downhill, downhill, thinning out, getting more good-natured, cleverer, more comfortable, more mediocre, more indifferent. . . . The sight of man is now a wearying sight—what is nihilism today is not this? . . . We are weary of man.[63]

For Nietzsche, the modern project fails. It has not produced an affirmation of life, just a meaninglessly rich society devoted to accumulation. Despite the Socratic and modern insistence that humankind no longer needs myth, this is exactly what the lost souls of modernity seek:

> Let us now think of the abstract man unguided by myth, the abstract education, the abstract morality, the abstract justice, the abstract state: let us picture to ourselves the lawless roving of the artistic imagination, unchecked by native myth: let us imagine a culture which has no fixed and sacred primitive seat, but is doomed to exhaust all its possibilities, and to nourish itself wretchedly on all other cultures—there we have the Present, the result of Socratism, which is bent on the destruction of myth. And now the mythless man remains eternally hungering amid the past, and digs and grubs for roots. . . . Let us ask ourselves whether the feverish and uncanny excitement of this culture is anything but the eager seizing and snatching at food of hungry man.[64]

Against hypercritical and nihilist modernity, we need a new myth and new instincts that affirm life in its fullness. This is what Nietzsche hoped for with Wagner, but it failed. As it should be clear by now, I do not take Nietzsche's break with Wagner to mean that he gives up on the dream of a new myth. Clearly, it continues in his unfulfilled promise to outline a "revalution of all values."[65] It must be a new myth that rejects both the accumulative logic of modernity and the cacophony of different instincts that result from it.

The Dual Structure of Contemporary Nihilism

We can now summarize and draw together Nietzsche's claims.

The world is an incomprehensible "sea of forces."[66] Myths greatly simplify the world and create an intelligible home for humans. This is not primarily intellectual, but embodied, instinctual knowledge. It is in our bodies, our language, and our practices. It makes the world intelligible, establishes how we relate to each other, tells us what is moral, how we should act, and so on. We are born into traditions that give us instincts. We never fully understand these instincts, and they make us social animals. We share these instincts with others, although they are never fully the same and never completely overlap.

Some instincts are better than others. Instincts can be healthy or unhealthy. Healthy instincts lead to human flourishing. This could be manifested in artistic accomplishments, great cities, great feats, outstanding people, and so on. Unhealthy instincts lead to human diminishment and withering away. Historically, traditions or cultures rise and fall. Not always, but often they begin with healthy instincts. With time, these instincts tend to become weakened and unhealthy.

In terms of instincts, Nietzsche characterizes modern life both as having unhealthy instincts and also as having instincts in disarray. At first, this may look contradictory, but it isn't. Nietzsche often relates the unhealthy instincts of modernity to values centered on money. He connects these to liberalism, utilitarianism, democracy, and the Socratic quest for eternal knowledge. Altogether, Nietzsche thinks contemporary consumer instincts are pathetic, and they make for miserable, sick humans—which Nietzsche characterized as the "last man."

Because the instincts of the last man are to destroy myth in the search for knowledge while simultaneously allowing for the proliferation and monetization of myths under capitalism, Nietzsche also characterizes modern consumer life as producing an "anarchy of . . . instincts."[67] Many now run around looking for meaning and purpose, without realizing that we have robbed ourselves of it. After

Nietzsche's madman announces the death of God, he realizes that he has come too early and no one has realized yet the situation we are in.

There is then, a certain core of instincts (which shape self-identity, social identity, morality, meaning, etc.) centered on productivity and accumulation (of money and knowledge). But these are unhealthy instincts that leave many unfulfilled and searching for meaning among the mounting debris of the destruction of cultures (the result of the "Socratic" rejection of myth) and the proliferation of new fantastic worlds and meanings (the result of the capitalist production of ever more things to be bought and sold, including new worlds and identities).

To be clear, according to Nietzsche, the modern world, the modern self, modern language, and modern morality are nihilistic because they center, on the one hand, on the accumulation of knowledge and, on the other, on the pathetic accumulation of money. The former destroys myth, worlds, and instincts. The latter tries to make a pretty penny by filling in the God-shaped holes left by the former with all sorts of things: new identities, new meanings, new loves, new pleasures, new joys. Together, they form a powerful instincts-killing machine. And, because they can only provide consumer goods—objects meant to be consumed and therefore temporary—they are ultimately empty and life denying.

Revaluation of All Values: Nietzsche's Fidelity to Myth

Nietzsche not only offers us a good picture of the dangers of cacophony, but his condemnation of both the nihilistic pecuniary core and the nihilistic "anarchy of instincts" helps us get a glimpse of the dual structure of contemporary cacophony.

For our purposes here, this will serve as a foundation for further analysis.

It is tempting to explore what exactly Nietzsche thought should be done about the problem of nihilism and how he would have dealt with cacophony. This question ends up being very complicated however and would take us too far afield from what we are trying to accomplish. With that said, it is worth flagging one issue in this regard that is relevant to the problem of cacophony.

Different scholars have offered different accounts of how Nietzsche seeks to escape nihilism. Unfortunately, as I mentioned earlier, Julian Young has argued the Anglophone tradition has tended to read Nietzsche in an individualistic manner.[68] On this reading, Nietzsche is often taken as something of a guide or model of an individual willing to experiment with different philosophies and ways of living, to try them on and see if they affirm life.[69] The emphasis here is on self-discovery and self-creation. The task of becoming an Übermensch is treated as an individual task.

Young worries that the generally accepted Anglophone story about the individualist Nietzsche misses the community and myth-oriented early Nietzsche of *The Birth of Tragedy*. Young wants to read later Nietzsche as still attempting to fulfill the dreams of the earlier Wagner-inspired Nietzsche—in other words, that the earlier community-inspired Nietzsche never goes away. The search for the Übermensch is not so much an individual quest but a quest for the founding of a new community.

While I think Young is correct, it is not my primary concern to try and resolve these differences. It should be clear from the discussion of instincts I have outlined here that I think Nietzsche firmly believes we are social creatures and that any solution to the problem of nihilism is primarily a social question.

What I want to point out is that the individualistic or liberal readings of Nietzsche tend to only have therapeutic, individualized solutions to the problem of nihilistic cacophony. While the individual may seek refuge, or joy, or some sort of solution to the problem of cacophony, this is not a resolution to the threat of cacophonous nihilism and the "anarchy of instincts." By not dealing with cacophony as a social problem, the individualist or liberal response risks exacerbating it. The fundamental cacophonous state is not challenged. Critically, this individualization of cacophony and conversion of it into a therapeutic or entrepreneurial problem subsumes it into the logic of consumerism. This problem will become clearer in Chapter 5.

Before turning to these questions, let us look at two more philosophers that warned us of the problem of cacophony, beginning with the increasingly forgotten Spanish philosopher Ortega y Gasset.

Notes

1 Blair is concerned with scholarly information. The concerns of this book are much broader than information. Blair, Ann M. *Too Much to Know: Managing Scholarly Information before the Modern Age* (New Haven, CT: Yale University Press, 2011).

2 In making this claim, I am following Hannah Arendt. See Arendt, Hannah. *The Human Condition* (Chicago: University of Chicago Press, 1998) and Pack, Justin. *How the Neoliberalization of Academia Leads to*

Thoughtlessness: Arendt and the Modern University (New York: Lexington Books, 2018).

3   This is the central claim of Julian Young's *Nietzsche's Philosophy of Religion* (New York, NY: Cambridge University Press, 2006), hereafter quoted as *NFR*. Young argues against what he takes to be the common Anglo-American reading of Nietzsche as a proponent of individualism. He seeks to show that Nietzsche is, if anything, a thinker of community. His argument hinges on paying attention to the intellectual and historical circumstances that surrounded and informed Nietzsche. Young argues that Nietzsche's philosophy of community (or religion) is obvious in his early works and lingers throughout his later works. This historical background I offer in this section draws from Young's work both in *Nietzsche's Philosophy of Religion* and his biography of Nietzsche entitled *Friedrich Nietzsche: A Philosophical Biography* (New York, NY: Cambridge University Press, 2010).

4   See for example Hobsbawm, Eric. *The Age of Capital: 1848–1875* (New York, NY: Vintage, 1996).

5   Nietzsche, Friedrich. *On the Future of Our Educational Institutions. The Complete Works of Friedrich Nietzsche, Vol. 3* (Edinburgh, Eng: Morrison and Gibb Limited, 1910), 12; hereafter cited as *FEI*, followed by page numbers.

6   Ibid., 136.

7   Ibid., 60, 42.

8   Ibid., 37.

9   More on this in the sections on myth and instincts.

10 Young, Julian. *Nietzsche's Philosophy of Religion* (New York, NY: Cambridge University Press, 2006).

11 Ibid., 220.

12 See Dennis J. Schmidt's humorously entitled *On Germans and Other Greeks* (Bloomington, IN: Indiana University Press, 2001) for a discussion of this.

13 See Young's historical overview in *NPR*.

14 *NPR*, 1.

15 Nietzsche, Friedrich. *The Gay Science* (New York, NY: Vintage, 1974), 228; hereafter cited as *GS*, followed by page numbers.

16 Ibid., 229.

17 Nietzsche, Friedrich *Beyond Good and Evil: Prelude to a Philosophy of the Future* (New York, NY: Vintage, 1989), 176; hereafter cited as *BGE*, followed by page numbers.

18 Ibid., 2.

19 Ibid., 3.

20 Nietzsche, Friedrich. *The Will to Power* (New York, NY: Vintage, 1968), 565; hereafter cited as *WP*, followed by page numbers.

21 Young, Julian, ed. *Individual and Community in Nietzsche's Philosophy* (NY: Cambridge University Press, 2012).

22 Nietzsche, Friedrich. *The Birth of Tragedy* (New York, NY: Dover, 1995), 8; hereafter cited as *BT*, followed by page numbers.

23 Ibid., 23.

24 Ibid., 22.

25 Ibid., 22.

26 Technically, he says these are drives of nature, and this whole process is one in which nature or will "plays with itself in the eternal fullness of its joy" (90). I do not need to elaborate on the metaphysics involved to understand the question of human flourishing, and Nietzsche later abandons this metaphysics.

27 *BT*, 1–3.

28 Ibid., 3.

29 Ibid., 6.

30 Ibid., 26.

31 Note that there is something artificial about separating these drives too radically. They are intertwined and related. Later, Nietzsche will cease talking about the Apollonian at all and subsume it into the Dionysian.

32 *BT*, 76.

33 Ibid., 21.

34 Ibid., 59.

35 Ibid., 85.

36 Ibid., 85.

37 *WP*, 9–10; see also Nietzsche, Friedrich. *The Genealogy of Morals* (New York, NY: Oxford University Press, 1999), 108–14.

38 *BT*, iv.

39 Ibid., 86.

40 Descartes, Rene. *Meditations on First Philosophy* (Cambridge, UK: Cambridge University Press, 1996).

41 *BT*, 23.

42 Ibid., 53.

43 *BGE*, 24.

44 *WP*, 270

45 *BGE* 26.

46 Ibid., 36.

47 *WP*, 271, 284.

48 Ibid., 550.

49 *BT*, 85.

50 *BGE*, 11.

51 Ibid., 53; I take the interesting phrase "mystagogue" to stress how Socrates condemns myth while attempting to establish a monopoly on it.

52 *BT*, 47.

53 Ibid., 23.

54 Nietzsche, Friedrich, *The Portable Nietzsche* (New York, NY: Penguin Books, 1977), 479.

55 *GS*, 85.

56 *BGE*, 157.

57 *GS*, 94.

58 Ibid., 259.

59 Nietzsche, Friedrich. *The Portable Nietzsche* (New York, New York: Penguin Books, 1977), 475.

60 *GS*, 181.

61 *WP*, 47.

62 Ibid., 44.

63 Nietzsche, Friedrich. *The Genealogy of Morals* (New York, NY: Oxford University Press, 1999), 28.

64 *BT*, 85.

65 Nietzsche, Friedrich. *The Portable Nietzsche* (New York, NY: Penguin Books, 1977), 466. *GS*, 181.

66 *WP*, 550.

67 Nietzsche, Friedrich. *The Portable Nietzsche* (New York, NY: Penguin Books, 1977), 475.

68 Young, Julian. *Nietzsche's Philosophy of Religion* (New York, NY: Cambridge University Press, 2006).

69 *GS*, 34.

2
Ortega y Gasset and the *Selva Selvaggia*

Nietzsche lived through the unification and modernization of Germany in 1871. In 1898, Spain lost its last colonies: Cuba, the Philippines, and Puerto Rico, in the Spanish American war. As a result, many in Spain began to question what had led to the decline of Spain from its imperial heights. Did Spain need to modernize like Germany and Italy? One of the leading intellectuals that wrestled with the question of Spanish modernization in this period was the philosopher José Ortega y Gasset.

Like Nietzsche, Ortega y Gasset was deeply concerned about the benefits and difficulties of modernization. Also like Nietzsche, he was quite critical of mass consumer culture. Unlike Nietzsche, however, Ortega y Gasset thought highly of "liberal democracy." With this said, he was deeply aware of the potential problems of liberalism. Because of his intense criticism of mass culture and the ways it tended to undermine liberal democracy, especially in his most famous work *The Revolt of the Masses*, Ortega y Gasset is often treated as a conservative. Oddly, while Nietzsche has become beloved by some liberals and leftists, including radical leftists, despite being more conservative than they read him, I would argue Ortega y Gasset is far more relevant to our contemporary state of cacophony than his conservative reputation may suggest.

Where Ortega y Gasset stands out from other European thinkers of his time is his central concern with the proliferation of information and multiplication of realities that result from the project of modernity. The cacophony that results stands in the way of his efforts to modernize Spain, and Ortega y Gasset makes it clear in multiple works that this is, for him, the problem of our time. While Nietzsche offers, to my mind, the most important critique of cacophony, Ortega y Gasset makes the task of integration of information—we could call this cacophony management—one of the most important fundamental social, political, and philosophical tasks of our time. While Nietzsche seeks an Übermensch to create a new tradition, Ortega y Gasset calls the management of cacophony the mission of the university and, making her a potential hero of counterhegemony, the mission of the librarian. Perhaps even more than Nietzsche, Ortega y Gasset is a thinker of cacophony.

The Selva Selvaggia

In *The Mission of the Librarian*, Ortega y Gasset argues that human society often dies from a surfeit rather than from poverty:

> Under one form or another, this has already happened several times in history. Man loses himself in his own wealth: his own

culture, proliferating like tropical vegetation around him, ends by smothering him ... Man cannot [afford to] be too rich; if an excess of facilities and possibilities are offered for his choice, he comes to grief among them; and confounded with possessions, he loses the sense of necessity.

This has been the perennial tragic destiny of the aristocracies: all of them finally degenerated because the excess of means and facilities atrophied their energies.[1]

The metaphor of humanity losing itself in the jungle it has created is repeated in many of Ortega's works. His concern is that human society can get strangled in its own success. As he puts it in the essay *Man as Technician*:

For this is the absurd situation at which we have arrived: the wealth of material means that present-day man can count on for his living surpasses by far that of all other ages and we are clearly aware of its superabundance. Yet we suffer from an appalling restlessness because we do not know what to do with it, because we lack imagination for inventing our lives.[2]

Successful societies always run the risk of creating so much wealth, so much knowledge, and so many possibilities for living that it can become overwhelming. In *Man and Crisis*, he argues: "For his part, the man who knows many things, the cultivated man, runs the risk of losing himself in the jungle of his own knowledge; and he ends up by nor knowing what his own genuine knowledge is."[3] And further on:

Man who is lost in complications aspires to save himself in simplicity—a universal return to nudity, a general call to rid oneself of, to retire from, to deny, all richness, complexity, and abundance. The present and the immediate past appear as bowed down with the excessive growths of their possibilities. One can think too many thoughts, want too many things, follow too many different types of life. Life is perplexity; the more possibilities there are in it, the more perplexed, the more painfully perplexed, is man.[4]

Ortega y Gasset believes humans live in a social world that provides us with preconceptual understandings and standards that guide human action. "Without realizing it, we find ourselves installed in that network of ready-made solutions for the problems of our lives."[5] He calls the social world that we are born into and assimilate "generations" and argues that "life is time."[6] Although he does not use the Nietzschean term, I believe it is fair to say he thinks we are bequeathed a set of instincts that help us organize and make our world coherent and comprehensible. In *Man and Crisis*, he argues that societies are either in a state of ascension or a state of crisis. "In the classic age, in the golden age, man believes he knows on what he can depend in regard to his surroundings: he has a system of convictions which are genuine and strong, a world before him which is transparent." Because he has established instincts, his world "contains a minimum of unresolved problems."[7]

When those instincts begin breaking down, humanity enters a period of crisis, of "excess vegetation of his own culture." This crisis of culture has three components: "(1) The ideas about things and the norms of behavior of which culture consists become too complicated and overreach man's intellectual and moral ability... (2) Those ideas and those norms lose their vigor, their liveliness, and their obviousness for the man who must make use of them. (3) Culture is no longer distributed with organic spontaneity and precision . . . higher culture is now injected mechanically, as it were, into the masses."[8] While culture or society is a kind of spontaneous event, Ortega y Gasset stresses the role humanity has in reproducing culture and civilization—especially the role of those in power, the elite, and the academy. Thus, while one cannot know completely the assumptions that guide our functioning in the world (as Nietzsche would say, we cannot make our instincts transparent without destroying them), we can know something of them, and we clearly promote certain ideas and approaches. This is what Ortega thinks holds together particular societies or cultures for their duration until they are finally overcome by their own proliferation. The current human crisis, however, is unlike all previous crises. Not only are we dealing with the *selva selvaggia*, the proliferation of knowledge, and possibilities that threatens to strangle humanity, but with the revolt of the masses. For the first time in history, the masses have risen to power and have started to set the agenda themselves.

The Revolt of the Masses is Ortega y Gasset's central work. It shows how the twentieth-century crisis of mass society is unique in world history. Since Ortega y Gasset is clearly critical of the rise of the masses, many find his work elitist and dismiss it on those grounds. This is a mistake—a closer look reveals that Ortega y Gasset intends *The Revolt of the Masses* and, indeed, his entire oeuvre to be ultimately democratic. Let us see then, what he thinks is the unique challenge of our times.

The Increase of Life

In *The Revolt of the Masses*, Ortega y Gasset begins his dissection of the mass man by pointing out there are simply more people everywhere than there used to be. In Spain, previous to the time of his writing (1930), the theaters were not overly full of people. Neither were the restaurants full of people who spilled out in large waiting lines. "The individuals who made up these multitudes existed, but not *qua* multitude."[9] There were many people spread all over the place, but they didn't exist as a multitude with the same desire to be at the same place all at the same time. Where did this crowd come from? How did it come together to form the masses?

Previously, these individuals all lived in their own little circles, on their own farms, in their own villages. They might not have even spoken the same dialect. But through scientific advancements, technology, and political developments, divisions among them have been broken down. Ortega points out that "Each portion of the earth is no longer shut up in its geometrical position, but for many purposes of human life act upon other proportions of the planet."[10] Barriers which previously kept the world divided and unaware of the infinite diversity are crumbling or no longer exist. While previously an individual was presented with limited possibilities, and hence had limited desires, humankind is now experiencing an increase of life. Life is more, much more than it ever was previously. China is no longer a faraway mysterious place, but a place to which I can travel in a day. Distance has been radically decreased. Democracy has opened the doors to all to experience all these possibilities.

This increase in life has peculiar effects. The modern individual "feels lost amid his own abundance. With more means at its disposal, more knowledge, more technique than ever, it turns out the world today goes the same way as the worst of worlds that have been; it simply drifts."[11]

This increase in life has "overflowed all the channels, principles, norms, ideals handed down by tradition."[12] The cacophony of the present drowns out the past. Previously, because there were no other options, to live meant to accept a set of possibilities, "limitations, obligations, dependence; in a word, pressure."[13] However, as Ortega y Gasset sees it, this is no longer the case:

> The world which surrounds the new man from his birth does not compel him to limit himself in any fashion, it sets up no veto in opposition to him; on the contrary, it incites his appetites, which in principle can increase indefinitely.[14]

These limitless possibilities result in individuals who are profoundly ignorant of history and ungrateful to it. The masses are always looking forward to what they can have, without looking backward to what has made what they seek possible. Life no longer makes a claim on them. Instead, the masses make a ceaseless series of claims on life. The mass is not just a group of people. It is the mentality of the individual who feels they have a right to all possibilities and approaches life without regard for history. Mass men "are those for whom to live is to be every moment what they already are, without imposing on themselves any effort toward perfection; mere buoys that float on the waves."[15]

The Noble Life and Barbarism

Ortega y Gasset contrasts the ease of mass society with the obligations forced on nobility. The noble are "those who make great demands on themselves, piling up difficulties and duties."[16] He argues that democracy originally meant that persons who had the ability to lead and direct were selected by the majority to lead and direct them. Excellence was recognized and rewarded. But Ortega y Gasset thinks democracy has become warped and instead is now the decree against excellence and leaders. Leaders must be just like everyone else. Any difference must be quashed.

The results of this turn against excellence and the demotion of democracy to a sanction of the mass man is "root ignorance of the very principles of civilization."[17] Ortega is concerned that as a result of this leveling of society to the lowest common denominator, no work is done toward assuring that basic humanity and civility will continue. Faith is placed in continuing technological control, and those who doubt the system are ignored. The mass feels entitled to an opinion on everything without having done the work necessary to have an opinion.[18] The mass men are intellectual hermits, entirely comfortable within themselves, ready to tell everyone how it is (since their opinion is equal to all), but unwilling to be told what to do or to let life make a claim on them. Vulgarity becomes a right.[19] This breakdown of barriers and acceptance of all is nothing less than barbarism—"the lack of standards to which an appeal can be made."[20]

There is a sense that no one is at fault for this massive shift. The increase in scientific know-how led to new technologies and improved life to such a point that the masses were freed. But these new technologies also opened up so many new possibilities that culture and civilization have been obscured in the cacophonous jungle that has arisen. The result is newly freed masses that lack instincts to guide them through the brave new world.[21]

What I affirm is that there is no culture where there are no standards to appeal. There is no culture where there is no acceptance of certain final intellectual position to which a dispute may be referred. There is no culture where economic relations are not subject to a regulating principle to protect interests involved. There is no culture where aesthetic controversy does not recognize the necessity of justifying the work of art.[22]

Stated simply, human society needs standards. Ortega y Gasset argues the Enlightenment sought to destroy old traditions and replace them with a new sense of rationality and justice, but has failed to establish such standards. Ortega y Gasset, while critical of the ontological and epistemological assumptions of the project of modernity, is nonetheless strongly in favor of the ideals of the Enlightenment. "Civilization is, before all, the will to live in common. A man is uncivilized, barbarian in the degree in which he does not take others into account. Barbariam is the tendency to disassociation."[23] In a statement that shows he is not a blanket elitist, Ortega y Gasset continues: "the loftiest endeavor towards common life is liberal democracy. It carries to the extreme the determination to have consideration for one's neighbor."[24] Liberal democracy seeks to find a way for people to live with each other despite our differences and to create a mutual civilization despite those differences. This means liberal democracy will always deal with the tension between the need for standards that unify and respect for differences that tend to pull groups apart. Liberal democracy is therefore a very difficult task: "It was incredible that the human species should have arrived at so noble an attitude, so paradoxical, so refined, so acrobatic, so anti-natural.

Hence, it is not to be wondered at that this same humanity should soon appear anxious to get rid of it."[25]

There is a sense, on the other hand, however, that there is someone at fault for the new barbarism. And this is the scholars and leaders of civilization who failed to understand what is needed to preserve it. They failed in their duty, Ortega says, because of the barbarism of specialization.

The Barbarism of Specialization

Because liberal democracy is an unnatural and difficult, although highly desirable form of civilization, it takes a lot of work to create. The kind of work that is needed is never finished because the tension between the needs for standards that unite and the need to respect differences constantly threatens to undermine any standards. The kind of sensitivity, caution, capability for reasoning, and generousness that is essential to liberal democracy has to be inculcated and developed. The revolt of the masses represents a failure in this regard. What caused this failure? It is precisely the same problem that affects the masses: lack of historical consciousness.

> Since present-day man , as soon as he opens his eyes to life, finds himself surrounded by a superabundance of technical objects and procedures forming an artificial environment . . . he will tend to believe that all these things are there in the same way as nature itself is there without further effort on his part: that aspirin and automobiles grow on trees like apples. That is to say, he may

easily lose sight of technology and of the conditions—the moral conditions—[that make such a civilization possible].²⁶

This historical ignorance is not only a challenge for the mass man. "Historical knowledge is a technique of the first order to preserve and continue a civilization already advanced." Unfortunately, the "most 'cultured' people today are suffering from incredible ignorance of history."²⁷ Not only the masses, but the scholars and leaders of society, the very individuals who conceived and implemented the project of modernity, have become lost in an ahistorical technicism. Even more than the masses, "this new barbarism is above all the professional man, more learned than ever before, but at the same time more uncultured—the engineer, the physician, the lawyer, the scientist."²⁸ All of these individuals are specialists, of course, and for Ortega y Gasset, they are barbarians.

Ortega y Gasset sees the technicism that pervades modern society as a result of "capitalism and experimental science."²⁹ Both require specialization to function most efficiently. "Specialization commences precisely at a period which gives to civilized man the title 'encyclopedic'."³⁰ As the project of modernity commenced, the massive attempt to discover all knowledge, scholars broke up into disciplines to cover the material. These scholars focus on minutiae in the effort to accurately describe their small proportion of the world, which will later be assembled into a complete map like a giant puzzle. "He even proclaims it as a virtue that he takes no cognizance of what lies outside the narrow territory specially cultivated by himself, and gives the name of 'dilettantism' to any curiosity for the general scheme of knowledge."³¹ For Ortega y Gasset, the problem is that it is precisely the general scheme of knowledge that is needed to give a clear picture of what we are doing. It is the general ideas—the kind that all scholars had to deal with when a more comprehensive form of knowledge was required from them—that are needed to establish and sustain a liberal democracy. Otherwise, the members of a democracy are left to sort through an ever-increasing amount of information that they increasingly cannot understand.

The scientific method has been so spectacularly successful in the natural sciences that it has become the standard for knowledge and, as a result, warped how the social sciences and humanities view their own studies. "The prodigious achievement of natural science in the direction of the knowledge of things contrasts brutally with the collapse of this same natural science when faced with the strictly human element. The human element escapes physico-mathematical reason as water runs from a sieve."[32] The social sciences and the humanities lose a great deal when they reduce humanity to a set of statistics. "Human life, it would appear then, is not a thing, has not a nature, and in consequence we must make up our minds to think of it in terms of categories and concepts that will be *radically* different form such as shed light on the phenomena of matter."[33] This is precisely the focus of much of Ortega y Gasset's oeuvre: to attempt to find an approach to the study of humanity that is radically different from the scientific method.

His major enemies in the task of creating a new historical approach to human life are precisely the barbarian specialists. "The specialist 'knows' very well his own tiny corner of the universe; he is radically ignorant of all the rest."[34] This wouldn't be a problem if the specialist stuck to his or her own area of study, but:

> In politics, in art, in social usages, in the other sciences, he will adopt the attitude of primitive, ignorant man . . . by specializing

him, civilization has made him hermetic and self-satisfied within his limitations; but this very inner feeling of dominance and worth will induce him to wish to predominate outside his speciality. The result is . . . [even though his is highly qualified] . . . he will behave in almost all spheres of life as does the unqualified, the mass-man.[35]

The highly qualified, cultured scholar of the project of modernity is so narrowly qualified that he or she knows much about very little and yet still feels qualified to lecture anyone on everything (or refuses to speak on anything except their little area of study). Indeed, Ortega argues, it is these scholars who are the greatest impediment to an intelligent and careful response to the malaise of modernity. "That state of 'not listening,' of not submitting to higher courts of appeal which I have repeatedly put forward as characteristic of the mass-man, reaches its height precisely in these partially qualified men."[36]

The increase in life leads to the necessity for specialization. In the face of the ever-increasing amount of knowledge and possibilities, the Renaissance man who moves adeptly through the sciences and humanities becomes not only an unprecedented difficult achievement, but a mocked ideal. The specialist, narrow-minded and confident, rules over non-specialists until a barbaric system full of experts arises. The result is not the neat division of labor that adds up to a coherent whole but a cacophony of experts.

What Now? Integration

So what can be done? For Ortega y Gasset there must always be some kind of culture, some kind of way of sorting the flux and making life comprehensible. "Barbarism is the absence of standards to which appeal can be made."[37] This does not imply that a society can exist without standards—no society can live in a vacuum. Rather, Ortega y Gasset is arguing that when instincts are in disarray and competing standards pull people in different directions, society is in a state of decay.[38] The increase in knowledge has led to awareness of different standards in other parts of the world and the necessity for specialization. "The new barbarism is above all the professional man, more learned than ever before, but at the same time more uncultured—the engineer, the physician, the lawyer, the scientist."[39] Science cannot be a standard for society. When it *is* made a standard for society, society effectively becomes a machine driving constantly for more efficiency above all. The ends of society are forgotten and the means perfected.

Culture requires the historical awareness that we saw the mass man lacks. It requires sensitivity to the big picture, to ethics and to the different pushes and pulls within society. It requires, in short, "the genius for integration . . . the construction of a whole."[40]

This, then, is what Ortega y Gasset thinks we need: integrators. An integrator is not a social scientist who discovers the truth and then imposes it on the masses. Rather, an integrator summarizes information and presents it to society to help them clarify the many options and possibilities in the world around them. An integrator is essentially a facilitator of democracy. Naturally, any summarization will involve simplification. "The vocation of teaching is actually one of concealing."[41] The teacher does not tell the students everything there is to know. That would take a lifetime. The teacher inevitably conceals some, perhaps much, information for the sake of clarity. But unlike a totalitarian system, the teacher always leaves windows open.

The teacher shows different possibilities and invites others to explore them. The teacher shows the landscape, points out certain features, and then invites others to explore.

Observe what he has to say about the mission of the librarian:

Every society of the West today needs a certain number of doctors, magistrates, soldiers, and librarians—to cure their citizens when sick, to administer justice to them, to defend them, and to make them read...

Furthermore, the librarian of the future must direct the nonspecialized reader through the *selva selvaggia* of books. He will be the doctor and the hygienist of reading. On this point also we find ourselves in a situation quite the reverse of that in 1800. Today people read too much. The condition of receiving without much effort, or even without any effort, the innumerable ideas contained in books and periodicals has accustomed the common man to do no thinking on his own account; and he does not think over what he has read, the only method of making it truly his own. In addition, there is that gravest and most radically negative character of the book, and we must dedicate our utmost effort of attention to it. A large part of today's terrible public problem proceeds from the fact that ordinary minds are full of ideas received in inertia, ideas half understood and deprived of their virtues. Ordinary minds are thus stuffed with pseudo-ideas. In this aspect of his profession, I imagine the librarian of the future as a filter interposed between man and the torrent of books.[42]

With respect to the university, Ortega's call to integration is a call to return to its roots. This is where the university has played a role in the past. In *The Mission of the University*, Ortega y Gasset argues, the university was "responsible for the vital ideas of a time."[43] Ideally the university serves as the location to think through the traditions and problems of a particular time period. The university has essentially always served some purpose along these lines: to improve life and help organize knowledge—in other words, to establish culture.

Unfortunately, with the rise of modern science, the university has increasingly "turned to inquiry and forgotten culture."[44] We have become so enamored of the scientific method that "in our age, the content of culture comes largely from science, but . . . culture is not science." Furthermore, "life cannot wait until the sciences may have explained" a particular problem.[45] Science cannot provide the kinds of narratives that humans need, nor the kind of analysis that addresses the human need for meaning.

The call for integration may seem a call for anti-democratic social manipulation—the kind of thing Foucault has taught us to be sensitive to. I don't want to pretend there aren't potential problems in what Ortega y Gasset proposes. But I want to stress that the problem of excess he outlines seems to indicate that democracy in mass society is already under attack from the kind of malignant growth we have been examining. For Ortega y Gasset, a functioning democracy requires some simplification, lest it become too overgrown to see clearly.

Conclusions

When Nietzsche declared that God was dead, it was not only because the project of modernity had destroyed belief in the Medieval God, but that it had failed to replace Him with a livable alternative. Instead of the heaven on earth it had promised, the project of modernity resulted in what Ortega calls the "bureaucratization of life."[46] The narratives that had driven Medieval Christianity were replaced by nationalism and utilitarian liberalism. The former was a major contributor to the First World War. The latter tends to turn into consumerism that constantly pumps out new products and can only provide momentary and selective distractions. It is not surprising, therefore, that some political figures decided to use what the project of modernity *had* provided, control over the material universe, to try and correct what it hadn't, spiritual fulfillment. In the twentieth century, both the advocates and critics of modernity watched as all the lofty ideals of Enlightenment were bent, broken, and manipulated, and the cruelest forms of "neutral" science were put to use for systematic, efficient killing. The rise of fascism, socialism, and the World Wars showed the potential for science to both control and destroy humanity. Enlightenment had produced a cruel double: totalitarianism.

With the Holocaust in the rearview mirror and nuclear bombs on the horizon, the spiritual malaise combined with the excess of power meant that not only a good human existence but human existence itself was on the line. After the rise of socialism and fascism, the concern with fragmentation and malignant proliferation of information that drove thinkers like Ortega y Gasset took a back seat to the more pressing concerns about totalitarianism.

I think it is time to reexamine the problems raised by Ortega y Gasset. This is not to put aside questions of totalitarianism, but rather to recognize consumer mass society as a very different kind of totalitarianism—one driven by the logic of consumption and pleasure.

It is within this context of the ever-producing consumer capitalism that Ortega y Gasset becomes relevant again.

As I mentioned at the end of the last section, to some, Ortega's call for integration may smack of censorship and social control. If the Enlightenment sought to kill the priests, it had to put someone or something in their place. Ortega y Gasset seems to be calling for the university and for librarians to take on the role of the guardians of culture. This, of course, sounds like Enlightenment pretension. It sounds like Lenin's attempt to create an intellectual vanguard to watch over the rest of us.

But I think this doesn't do justice to the problem Ortega is pointing to. Ortega's question concerns how we create and preserve civilization in the face of the ever-increasing products, narratives, and information produced in the modern world. Ideally, we would do so democratically. But, as we have seen, Ortega is concerned that a functioning democracy is constantly threatened by the jungle of consumer capitalism. Here I think he is right—consumer capitalism encourages us to be consumers and make decisions as consumers, but democracy requires we be citizens and make decisions as citizens. The constant danger in a society that wants to be capitalistic and democratic is that the latter seems to be undermined by the former. It is much easier to be a consumer than a competent and active citizen.

What I am suggesting is that a generous reading of Ortega y Gasset would see his call for integrators as the recognition of the need for constant work to be done to establish functioning democracies or coherent traditions. This would not be the Enlightenment task of bringing the truth to the masses, but something more like the task of attempting to make the world the type of place in which citizens could make informed decisions. This would involve articulating what the social and political options are for and with citizens—not in a fashion that closes conversation, but in a fashion that encourages it. As such, we should read Ortega y Gasset alongside other figures like Dewey and Habermas.

Notes

1. Ortega y Gasset, José. *The Mission of the Librarian* (Boston, MA: G.K. Hall, 1961), 15–16.
2. Ortega y Gasset, José. *History as a System and Other Essays Toward a Philosophy of History* (New York, NY: Norton and Company, 1961), 121.
3. Ortega y Gasset, José. *Man and Crisis* (New York, NY: Norton and Company, 1958), 110.
4. Ibid., 142.
5. Ibid., 26.
6. Ibid., 42.
7. Ibid., 102.
8. Ibid., 128.
9. Ortega y Gasset, José. *The Revolt of the Masses* (New York, NY: Norton and Company, 1991), 13.
10. Ibid., 138.
11. Ibid., 44.
12. Ibid., 47.
13. Ibid., 56.
14. Ibid., 58.
15. Ibid., 15.
16. Ibid., 15.

17 Ibid., 67.
18 Ibid., 68.
19 Ibid., 70.
20 Ibid., 72.
21 Here I want to push Ortega y Gasset more in the direction of "instincts" than "standards"—the former term does much more work to move us away from Cartesianism.
22 Ibid., 72.
23 Ibid., 76.
24 Ibid., 76.
25 Ibid., 76.
26 Ibid., 143.
27 Ibid., 91.
28 Ortega y Gasset, José. *The Mission of the University* (New York, NY: Norton and Company, 1944), 58.
29 Ibid., 107.
30 Ibid., 110.
31 Ibid., 110.
32 Ortega y Gasset, José. *History as a System and Other Essays Toward a Philosophy of History* (New York, NY: Norton and Company, 1961), 185.
33 Ibid., 186.
34 Ortega y Gasset, José. *The Revolt of the Masses* (New York: Norton and Company, 1991), 111.
35 Ibid., 112.
36 Ibid., 113.
37 Ibid., 72.
38 Yet again I have chosen to use Nietzsche's language of "instincts" instead of Ortega's language of "standards."
39 Ortega y Gasset, José. *The Mission of the University* (New York, NY: Norton and Company, 1944), 58.

40 Ibid., 91.

41 Ibid., 69.

42 Ortega y Gasset, José. *The Mission of the Librarian* (Boston, MA: G.K. Hall, 1961), 154.

43 Ortega y Gasset, José. *The Mission of the University* (New York, NY: Norton and Company, 1944), 63.

44 Ibid., 89.

45 Ibid., 89.

46 Ortega y Gasset, José. *The Revolt of the Masses* (New York: Norton and Company, 1991), 121.

3

Hannah Arendt and *Amor Mundi*

Nietzsche helps us see the dual structure of cacophony: the nihilistic supernova effect and the nihilist core of *homo economicus*. Ortega y Gasset focuses on the resulting need for cacophony management. In this chapter, I want to turn to a third author who is also deeply concerned with these issues: Hannah Arendt. Arendt is helpful to this analysis for two reasons. First, she builds on and responds directly to Nietzsche, originally seeking to name arguably her most important book *Amor Mundi*—a direct response to Nietzsche's concept of *amor fati*. Second, her response is centered on the negative effects of cacophony on what she calls "worlds." In doing this, she moves the focus away from the individual effects of cacophony to their social and political effects. This is particularly helpful to push back against individualist readings of Nietzsche and thinkers related to him.

In this chapter, I will begin with Nietzsche's discussion of *amor fati* and Arendt's revision of this in her term *amor mundi*. Since Arendt's focus is not on *fate*, but on *world*, I will have to explain what she means by "world." Then I will examine the relation of cacophony to the world.

Amor Fati and Eternal Recurrence

In a well-known passage from *The Gay Science*, Nietzsche offers a thought experiment:

> What if some day or night a demon were to steal into your loneliest loneliness and say to you: "This life as you now live it and have lived it you will have to live once again and innumerable times again; and there will be nothing new in it, but every pain and every joy and every thought and sigh and everything unspeakably small or great in your life must return to you, all in the same succession and sequence—even this spider and this moonlight between the trees, and even this moment and I myself. The eternal hourglass of existence is turned over again and again, and you with it, speck of dust!" Would you not throw yourself down and gnash your teeth and curse the demon who spoke thus? Or have you once experienced a tremendous moment when you would have answered him: "You are a god, and never have I heard anything more divine." If this thought gained power over you, as you are it would transform and possibly crush you; the question in each and every thing, "Do you want this again and innumerable times again?" would lie on your actions as the heaviest weight! Or how well disposed would you have to become to yourself and to life to long for nothing more fervently than for this ultimate eternal confirmation and seal?[1]

This famous challenge is known as the myth of eternal recurrence: what if when you die, you live again the same life you are now living? Would you want to do so, or would this feel like a curse? Ultimately, this question concerns how we are reacting to life. Do we love it? Or are we caught up in some sort of life denial that causes us to hate our life or tire of it? The latter case would be a state of nihilism or nothing-ism.

The myth of eternal recurrence is often interpreted as an individual challenge, especially by the Anglo-American tradition. This is not wrong, as long as we keep in mind Nietzsche's interest in establishing thriving communities. Viewed through this lens, it is a call for new Übermensch—new potential founders of thriving communities. But is also, and likely primarily, a measuring stick for entire traditions. An individual can use it to think about how they are living their own life, but for Nietzsche, it is also to measure whether a tradition is thriving or wilting.

Nietzsche is not naïve. He recognizes that life can be nasty, brutish, mean, and short. Bad things happen. What he wants to know is do we embrace life as a whole, with all the highs and lows this involves:

> I want to learn more and more to see as beautiful what is necessary in things as what is beautiful in them—thus I will be one of those who make things beautiful. *Amor fati*: let that be my love from now on! I do not want to wage war against ugliness. I do not want to accuse; I do not even want to accuse the accusers. Let looking away be my only negation. And, all in all on the whole: someday I wish to be only a Yes-sayer![2]

Historically, different traditions have tried to deal with the ugly and painful aspects of life in different ways. Christianity and Plato, for example, suggest another realm exists, heaven or the realm of forms, where pain and imperfections do not exist. We can take comfort looking toward, modeling ourselves on, or escaping to this perfect realm. Other traditions like Stoicism and Buddhism try to teach us to be impervious to or at least control how we react to ugliness and pain. Another tradition, the project of modernity, often seeks to eliminate or minimize pain and suffering.

For Nietzsche, all of these approaches are doomed to fail because they deny fundamental aspects of life in one way or another. Not only can the pain and ugliness not be eliminated, it would be a disaster for human experience if they were:

> But what if pleasure and displeasure are so intertwined that whoever *wants* as much as possible of one *must* also have as much as possible of the other—that whoever wants to learn to "jubilate up to the heavens" must also be prepared for "grief unto death"? . . . .
>
> Even today you still have the choice: either as little displeasure as possible, in short, lack of pain . . . or as much displeasure as possible as the price for the growth of a bounty of refined pleasures and joys that hitherto have seldom been tasted. Should you decide on the former, i.e. if you want to decrease and diminish people's susceptibility to pain, you also have to decrease and diminish their capacity for joy.[3]

Clearly in this last passage, Nietzsche's target is modernity and utilitarianism, the primary ethics of modernity. For Nietzsche, the utilitarian desire to create the greatest amount of pleasure for the greatest amount of people and the inverse principle that seeks to decrease suffering as much as possible for as many people as possible is critically misguided. The highs only have meaning in the context of the lows. If we are always seeking to eliminate the lows, we essentially will cut off our ability to feel deeply, and we will also hamstring our ability to feel the highs.

Nietzsche's concern with the leveling that occurs in modernity is not limited to utilitarianism but extends to his concerns about democracy and science. Take for example the following criticism of the "'scientific' interpretation of the world":

> What? Do we really want to permit existence to be degraded for us like this—reduced to a mere exercise for a calculator and an indoor diversion for mathematicians? Above all, one should not wish to divest existence of its *rich ambiguity* . . . an interpretation that permits counting, calculation, weighing, seeing, and touching and nothing more—that is a crudity and a naiveté, assuming that it is not a mental illness, an idiocy . . . A "scientific" interpretation of the world, as you understand it, might therefore still be one of the *most stupid* of all possible interpretations of the world, meaning that it is one of the poorest in meaning . . . an essentially mechanical world would be an essentially *meaningless* world. Assuming that one estimated the *value* of a piece of music according to how much it could be counted, calculated and expressed in formulas: how absurd would such a "scientific" estimation of music be! What would one have comprehended, understood, grasped of it? Nothing, really nothing of what is "music" in it![4]

In this passage, Nietzsche criticizes scientific interpretations of the world that simplify the world in ways that strip from it the "rich ambiguity" of life. We need to be careful here, because, as we saw in Chapter 1, Nietzsche does think that we humans need to make sense of life and that this has been done traditionally through the creation of "myths." If we don't have some way of reducing the immense and confusing richness of life to comprehensible patterns, which we saw Nietzsche calls the "mythical maternal home," we would be constantly overwhelmed and lost.[5] So his criticism is not necessarily of efforts to simplify the world which is "a monster of energy . . . a sea of forces flowing and rushing together, eternally changing, eternally flooding back . . . ,"[6] but against efforts which "divest existence of its *rich ambiguity*." This is the accusation Nietzsche makes against Socrates and the entire tradition he thinks Socrates initiated. This is a tradition that seeks to definitively describe reality—in other words, to fully understand reality so that there is nothing left unknown. Nietzsche thinks not only that this is impossible but that it has the effect of eliminating ambiguity and leaving the world withered and two-dimensional. For Nietzsche, modern science strips the world of meaning. This is not a criticism of science per se—it is how science works. The mistake is taking science to be describing all of reality as opposed to, say, just the physiological aspects of reality. If we make this mistake, we end up with a mechanical, meaningless world.

To thrive, Nietzsche argues, we must embrace all of life. We must love our fate (*amor fati*) so much that we would be excited to repeat our life over and over again. If we find this possibility dreadful, or a tradition in general finds this possibility dreadful, this would be a key sign of nihilism. The ideal of *amor fati* and the myth of eternal recurrence are both tools to diagnose nihilism, but also function as solutions to it. For those who read Nietzsche through a personal and/or individualistic lens, *amor fati* is an ideal of self-improvement. For the more communitarian reading, it is a way to judge and reform communities.

Amor Mundi

Arendt is often read in conversation with her famous teacher Martin Heidegger, but it is clear she is also responding to Nietzsche. She originally wanted to give the book *The Human Condition* the title *Amor Mundi*, but her editor thought that would not be understood by many readers and instead suggested the current title. Her desire to use the title *Amor Mundi* is a bit surprising because, at first glance, the book does not seem to be about the love of the world (or, as we will see, *a* world). Moreover, without the title *Amor Mundi*, readers may not realize that Arendt is giving both an alternative account of nihilism and an alternative solution to it. I have written a book-length treatment exploring what she means by *amor mundi* and comparing and contrasting this with a similar concept in Native American thought.[7] I will offer a condensed version of those arguments as needed here.

Clearly, Arendt is responding to and building on Nietzsche with her concept of *amor mundi*. But, like her teacher Heidegger, Arendt was worried about the individualistic bent of modern society and, in terms of philosophy, in early twentieth-century existentialism.[8] By shifting the language from "fate" to "world," Arendt is moving the focus from the potential individualistic readings of Nietzsche back toward something more social.

But what does Arendt mean by world? In everyday language, world is often used synonymously with Earth. While Arendt eventually distinguishes "world" from "Earth," she opens the text discussing our modern alienation from the world/Earth. Specifically, she looks at the response to the launch of Sputnik in 1957 and says that "the immediate reaction, expressed on the spur of the moment, was relief about the first 'step toward escape from men's imprisonment on Earth.'"[9] This is not, she thinks, merely side commentary from a particular American reporter, but a common sentiment that is summarized by the following statement from the gravestone of a Russian scientist: "Mankind will not remain bound to the Earth forever."[10]

Seeing this antipathy toward the world/Earth, she asks: "Should the emancipation and secularization of the modern age, which began with a turning-away, not necessarily from God, but from a god who was the Father of men in heaven, end with an even more fateful repudiation of an Earth who was the Mother of all living creatures under the sky?"[11] Arendt adds here to Nietzsche's death of God, the death of or at least alienation from Mother Earth. The world/Earth is of course necessary for human existence and yet modern man has initiated "a rebellion against human existence as it has been given, a free gift from nowhere (secularly speaking), which he wishes to exchange, as it were, for something he has made himself."[12]

She finishes the prologue with the claim that *The Human Condition* seeks to "trace back modern world alienation, its twofold flight from the Earth into the universe and from the world into the self, to its origins."[13] Here she begins to distinguish Earth from world. In fact, she basically drops discussing Mother Earth and Earth alienation and instead, for the rest of the text, focuses primarily on world alienation.

To explain what she means by "world," Arendt turns to ancient Greece and the difference between the private and public realms. On her reading, for the ancient Greeks, the private realm refers to the domestic sphere and the activity of labor. Labor consists of those activities that are related to biological necessity: cooking, cleaning, making clothing, raising children, and other activities associated with home economics (the managing of a household). These tasks are never finished and can be quite onerous due to their repetitive nature.

Some Greeks, those that were wealthy enough and had the status of citizens, could leave the backstage of the private realm and enter the main stage of the public realm. Here they could participate with other free men in the "world" of the *polis*:

> ... the term "public" signifies the world itself, in so far as it is common to all of us and distinguished from our privately owned place in it. This world, however, is not identical with the Earth or with nature. ... It is related, rather, to the human artifact, the fabrication of human hands, as well as to affairs which go on among those who inhabit the man-made world together. To live together in the world means essentially that a world of things is between those who have it in common, as a table is located between those who sit around it; the world, like every in-between, relates and separates men at the same time.[14]

"World," in her technical sense, is not the Earth, but a space of meaning and community created by humans. It has a material component: the buildings, temples, monuments, art, the structure of the city itself, the landscape, and so on. When we speak of the "world" of Rome, we think of the city of Rome, the Colosseum, the Pantheon, the well-built roads, gladiators, wine, Garum, olives, Roman cement, Roman coins, Roman clothing, the backdrop of the Italian countryside. All the different aspects of the physical world of Rome embody and are suffused in different ways with the moral, spiritual, social, political, and aesthetic aspects of "Rome." Stoic austerity, the many gods, the cruel patriarchy and institution of slavery, Empire, the styles of Roman architecture, the imitation of Greek sculpture, and so on. All of this together makes a "world," in this case the "world" of Rome.

We can experience worlds. Different worlds have different cultures, customs, aesthetics, moralities, philosophies, and moods. Toyko is its own world, as is Guanajuato (Mexico), and San Francisco, and rural Argentina, and Cairo, and the Grand Palace in Bangkok. Much of tourism is essentially the consumption of different worlds.

Historically, Arendt thinks, worlds were sources of meaning and identity. Athenians wanted to leave the private sphere for the freedom to participate in the glory of Athens. Here one could accomplish recognition and honor by contributing to the glory of the city through military accomplishments or great speeches and acts. The greatest citizens were immortalized and associated with their cities (Solon, Pericles, Socrates, etc.):

> The *polis* was supposed to multiply the occasions to win "immortal fame," that is to multiply the chances for everybody to distinguish himself, to show in deed and word who he was in his unique distinctness. One, if not the chief, reason for the incredible development of gift and genius in Athens, as well as for the hardly less surprising swift decline of the city-state, was precisely that from beginning to end its foremost aim was to make the extraordinary an ordinary occurrence of everyday life. The second function of the *polis* . . . was to offer a remedy for the futility of action and speech; for the chances that a deed deserving fame would not be forgotten, that it actually would become "immortal," were not very good.[15]

A world is not something we create (as if from scratch), but something we remake, *preserve*, and defend. For those who love their world, it is a work of art that they have been gifted by those who went before, and they have a wonderful chance to add to its glory. If they do so, they will be remembered by those to come after them. A "world," then, connects generations across time and anchors them together to a place. Understood in this way, we can see why it would make sense to speak of *amor mundi*. It means to love one's ancestors, one's culture, one's food, one's tradition, future generations tied to that world, the art, the temples, the gods, the smells . . . !

Amor mundi is not unique to the ancient Greeks and Romans. The same sort of love of a particular world is evident in many Native American traditions.[16] It was likely present in every world. With that said, that does not mean that everyone in a particular world would have loved their world. It is easy to be enthusiastic about a world if you are benefiting from it. Women in Athens could not become citizens and thus could never be free. Similarly, Athens, like Rome later, relied on slave labor. There were many in the axial age who critiqued their own times and their own worlds. Furthermore, various axial traditions (Greece, Israel, China, India) were founded by warrior cultures, some of which were highly critical of early agricultural civilizations—the most famous being the Biblical condemnation of the "whore of Babylon." We could add to this the many indigenous critiques of "civilizations."[17]

Amor mundi was not universal and not simple. Obviously, one could love one world while hating another. Arendt has multiple reasons for invoking it, but the primary thing that interests us here is her efforts to move the analysis of nihilism away from modern individualism and the seeming solipsism of existentialism toward an *amor fati* that includes worlds.

Modern World Alienation

By reframing the question of nihilism from the failure of *amor fati* to the failure of *amor mundi*, Arendt shifts the issue from individual *ennui* and *anomie* to modern world alienation. This has both historical causes and ideological causes.

Arendt identifies three historical causes of modern world alienation:

> Three great events stand at the threshold of the modern age and determine its character: the discovery of America and the ensuing exploration of the whole Earth; the Reformation, which by expropriating ecclesiastical and monastic possessions started the two fold process of individual expropriation and the accumulation of social wealth; the invention of the telescope and the development of a new science that considers the nature of the Earth from the viewpoint of the universe.[18]

The first event Arendt points to is the "discovery of America and the ensuing exploration of the whole Earth." This had the effect of expanding human understanding far beyond the traditional constraints of a few neighboring worlds:

> the mapping of her lands and the charting of her waters ... man has taken full possession of his mortal dwelling place and gathered the

infinite horizons, which were temptingly and forbiddingly open to all previous ages, into a globe whose majestic outlines and detailed surface he knows as he knows the lines in the palm of his hand.[19]

Eventually this leads to the "abolition of distance" and the "shrinkage of space" through modern trains, planes, cars, and boats.[20] This is obviously a radical change to human identity, understanding, and ethics.[21] Examining this in detail would go far beyond what we can do here, but the basic effect of bursting the traditional boundaries of worlds should be clear.

The second event she points to is the Reformation and the resulting expropriation. This broke apart the medieval Catholic worlds and led to a fragmentation and proliferation of religious traditions. Arendt claims that premodern identity was tied to a particular world. In a very real sense, one belonged to that world. Thus, Arendt claims to own a home in Rome was much less like modern home ownership and more like being owned by Rome. The home was a part of Rome, and if you lived there, you had duties to Rome itself. In premodernity, many or most non-slaves belonged to their world. But the process of expropriation initiated "the complete separation of the laborers from all property."[22] This expelled peasant farmers who had owned and been owned by particular land out of these places and led to homeless proletariats that were forced to move to cities and begin working in factories. The "freeing" of markets initiated a logic of tearing humans from their worlds and sucking them into the machinery of accumulation.

The last event she mentions is the "development of a new science" and the rejection of the "testimony of nature."[23] Here Arendt has in mind the scientific revolution and the ways it caused us to doubt our experience of the external world and instead rely on instruments that revealed both a micro-cosmos and the incomprehensibly large universe. This displaces humans much further than the exploration of the Earth and expropriation. As knowledge of the micro-cosmos and universe proceeds, the language used to understand them becomes increasingly mathematical and specialized, essentially becoming incommunicable to non-specialists.[24] This proliferation of languages also proliferates realities—or perspectives of reality—undermining the common sense that exists in a particular world.[25] Ultimately we are left without a mutually comprehensible world: "What men now have in common is not the world, but the structure of their minds."[26]

In addition to the historical causes of modern world alienation that Arendt analyzes, there is also a fundamental ideological shift that is central to her claims. In *The Human Condition*, Arendt distinguishes between three types of activities: labor, work, and action. Each has an associated type of person: *animal laborans*, *homo faber*, and *homo politicus*. As we saw earlier, by labor, Arendt means the repetitive tasks associated with the basic conditions of life—the sorts of things associated with home economics. The Greeks did not value these tasks and instead were interested in escaping them for the *bios politikos*— the life of freedom in the *polis*. It is here that one can engage in "action" activity free from coercion and necessity. Great actions can become immortalized. This is where *homo faber* comes into the picture. *Homo faber* builds the world by making statues, art, buildings, boats, temples—the physical things that have a permanent or semi-permanent status. The labor of *animal laborans* is constantly eaten up, used for the continuance of life, but the work of *homo faber* is much more permanent. Interestingly, the free citizens of the polis need *homo faber* to help immortalize great actions and build a permanent world, but they also want to prevent the instrumental and utilitarian logic of *homo faber* from infiltrating the free logic of the polis.[27] Thus, in terms of a value hierarchy, *homo politicus* and action are the most important and most desirable, *homo faber* and work are highly important and yet less desirable because they are unfree, and *animal laborans* and labor are denigrated as deeply unfree, full of drudgery, and endless.

The reason Arendt goes into such theoretical detail in her account of the ancient Greek world is because she thinks these values have become inverted in modernity. The very short version of this shift is as follows:

1. Freedom, action, and the *vita activa* are the highest forms of life in ancient Greece. Work and labor make this possible for the lucky few.

2. The *vita contemplativa* becomes ascendant in late antiquity and the medieval era as the focus shifts to finding peace (*ataraxia*) and/or growing close to God through contemplation.

3. The project of modernity returns to the *vita activa*, but not with an emphasis on freedom and action (in Arendt's sense of these terms). Since modernity is interested in creating new modern worlds and new modern states, it places the emphasis on *homo faber*, work, and making.

4. Eventually, however, modernity has come to value the promise of abundance that comes from labor and has

increasingly embraced the logic of the endless production of consumer goods. Our new consumerist modernity has entrenched consumer "freedom" and forgotten the freedom of action, and has also lost the concern with permanence that comes with *homo faber* and work in favor of the profitability of (and the promise of the alleviation of suffering through) consumer "abundance." As Arendt puts it: "The ideals of *homo faber*, the fabricator of the world, which are permanence, stability, and durability, have been sacrificed to abundance, the ideal of *animal laborans*."[28]

The genealogy Arendt offers is meant to show the inversion from the priority of action over work and labor in the ancient Greek world to the priority of labor over work and action in the modern world. For Arendt, this is a disaster on multiple levels and key to understanding modern nihilism.

Nihilism, World and Meaning

Nietzsche proposes *amor fati* as the antidote to nihilism. We can read backward from the concept of *amor fati* to understand what Nietzsche means by nihilism: if *amor fati* is the love of life including the bad parts, then nihilism is the hatred or denial of life due to the rejection of those parts of life we dislike. Arendt proposes *amor mundi* as the antidote to nihilism. If we read backward from the concept of *amor mundi*, can we get an idea of what nihilism is for Arendt? Not quite. It would seem that the opposite of *amor mundi* is the hatred of a world.

And indeed, this is what Arendt seems to be pointing at with her opening discussion of Sputnik and the enthusiasm to leave Mother Earth. The Earth and her gifts are the basis of the human condition, and yet, Arendt finds an alarming desire to escape these bounds. This could be construed as hatred of our human condition.

But Arendt proceeds to analyze not Earth alienation but world alienation. Her analysis shows historical events at the outset of modernity that destroyed medieval worlds and eventually enthroned the logic of labor and abundance. By rejecting *homo faber* and work in favor of *animal laborans* and labor, the permanence and durability of work is exchanged for the abundance of labor. But with this abundance comes a qualitative shift toward impermanence and fragility. This effects the quality of the objects in the world around us: we are increasingly surrounded by mass produced consumer goods that do not last long. This is not limited to our food, our clothing, our possessions, but also our houses, our workplaces, our cities—to cut to the chase, if the world is made of fragile things, then the world too becomes fragile.

Why is this fragilization of worlds so dangerous for Arendt? Here we can get help from Julian Young. In *The Death of God and the Meaning of Life*. Young looks at various responses to the crisis of nihilism from nineteenth- and twentieth-century continental thinkers. With regard to twentieth-century figures, including early Heidegger, Sartre, Camus, Foucault, and Derrida, Young argues they tend to seek solutions that are rooted in individual choice and responsibility. Each individual now has the task of making meaning for themselves. This can be a daunting task, but it is also one that allows each person to take responsibility for themselves and their own lives. Young argues that while this may appear liberating, any such response to the problem of nihilism will fail, because if we choose our own meaning in life, we will always know that the only force behind it is our own choice. It is not a calling that comes from without, but an ultimately arbitrary preference. He argues that of these thinkers, only later Heidegger offers a vision of meaning we must take up that is not a matter of preference, the task of "guardianship."[29] We don't need to examine here what exactly Young means by "guardianship" and whether he is correct. For our purposes, what matters is his claim that it is critically important that meaning cannot be sufficiently strong enough unless we experience it as coming from without. It could be argued that later Heidegger is not alone in seeking for a meaning that comes forcefully from without and compels us. Levinas clearly has this kind language.[30] It has been argued that this kind of calling is also critical for Derrida.[31] My claim here is that Arendt agrees with her teacher Heidegger that meaning will only have a sufficient hold on us if it comes from without.

Traditionally, meaning comes from a world. It is given by a world that predates us and connects us to a community. If this world is experienced as a good world and the meaning a particular individual is given in the world is fulfilling, then it will be experienced as a gift. I may be born into a family of carpenters and see such a task as being meaningful and fulfilling in a particular world. Of course, if a world is experienced as bad, then a given set of meanings and roles may be experienced as a curse. The idea that meaning is tied to a world does not have to be romanticized.

The destruction of the medieval worlds at the outset of modernity doesn't result in worldlessness. These worlds didn't simply vanish but morphed into new modern worlds. The problem is that these new modern worlds are fragile. This means that meanings offered by any such world are also fragile. Many scholars have noted the proliferation of worlds in modernity and the ways that humans increasingly live in multiple worlds and move in and out of worlds more often.[32] For example, imagine a person born into a Catholic family in Ohio. They grow up making sense of the world and finding purpose through a Catholic lens. They may enjoy meeting with other practitioners and participating in youth activities with other Catholics. Their world could also be an agricultural one. Maybe their town is deeply excited by American football, and many love the Ohio State football and people are divided by devotion to the Bengals or the Browns. Say they go off to college in New York and become introduced to a very different world. They may fall in love with the big city. They could study art and get immersed in that world. But then they graduate and end up joining the Peace Corps, spending time in Kenya and immersing themselves in that world. Like many of us in modernity, over the course of a lifetime, they are moving in and out of worlds, finding meaning in different ways over time, committing to different life projects. They could lose their childhood religious faith and become Buddhists. They may become committed to politics and find meaning fighting for a political cause.

The point is not necessarily that life was more meaningful in premodernity when there were fewer worlds and less movement between worlds. Again, there were clearly people in premodernity that hated and criticized particular worlds. Rather, Arendt is describing the fragility of modern worlds and the fragility of modern meaning. She clearly is worried that the accelerating consumer logic means we will consume our way through world after world in a most often fruitless search for meaning and purpose.

The proliferation of worlds corresponds to the cacophonous supernova effect, but there is at the heart of this explosion a "stable" core. If the supernova for Arendt is, among other things, a proliferation of worlds, the core is what she calls "the society of jobholders." We can think of the proliferation of worlds as what we get to do after work and on the weekends, and the core as our everyday work. Arendt is not kind about this core:

> The last stage of the laboring society, the society of jobholders, demands of its members a sheer automatic functioning, as though individual life had actually been submerged in the overall life process of the species and the only active decision still required of the individual were to let go, so to speak, to abandon his individuality, the still individually sense pain and trouble of living, and acquiesce in a dazed, "tranquilized," functional type of behavior. The trouble with modern theories of behaviorism is not that they are wrong but that they could become true, that they actually are the best possible conceptualization of certain obvious trends in modern society. It is quite conceivable that the modern age—which began with such an unprecedented and promising outburst of human activity—may end in the deadliest, most sterile passivity history has ever known.[33]

Here we find the most Nietzsche-like description of modern nihilism in *The Human Condition*. This is Arendt's version of Nietzsche's "last man"—the thoughtless, vacuous, empty shell of a modern human. This is what we could become (or perhaps already are?). It is worth pointing out that while this could be thought of as only applying to the 9–5 grind of the workday, from which we escape (TGIF!) to the "freedom" of the weekend and our evenings, the "freedom" of choice in our time off is just as vacuous and particularly insidious because it covers over the nihilistic core of jobholding. Playing and consuming in the supernova deludes us into thinking we are in a good place.

The Onslaught of the New

In an essay on education, Arendt makes the following claim:

> The responsibility for the development of the child turns in a certain sense against the world: the child requires special protection and care so that nothing destructive may happen to him from the world. But the world, too, needs protection to keep it from being overrun and destroyed by the onslaught of the new that bursts upon it with each new generation.[34]

This passage is very helpful and introduces the spectacular phrase "the onslaught of the new." The first part of this claim is straightforward. Child need protection from the world. Some things are better for them to experience when they are older (or not at all). But for our purposes here, we are interested in the reverse: protecting the world from "the onslaught of the new."

At first blush, the idea that new generations are a threat to a world seems like a grumpy conservative complaint. But Arendt is no curmudgeon pining for the past. On the contrary, she is obsessed with revolution, as we can see in *On Revolution*. What Arendt wants is a good world. But under the logic of *animal laborans* (labor and abundance), all worlds are under the threat of consumption. If we were able to bring about a new world that encourages human flourishing, it is hard to imagine how it would not just be gobbled up or forgotten in the proliferation of worlds.

This raises, I think, terribly underappreciated questions about the ethics of production. Take, for example, academic production. Academics are under intense pressure to publish or perish. The resulting culture of frantic production is not only absurd but alarmingly inhumane.[35] While there is some criticism of neoliberal academic culture, the machinery of academic production is so powerful and has such momentum that none of these criticisms seem to register.[36] There is an immense thoughtlessness here, and everyone is in such a hurry to win the game of academic production that no one seems to wonder about whether we should.

But Arendt gives us the resources to think about why more and newer are not necessarily better, but actually an engine that can drive world alienation and nihilism. A world is a reduction of the incomprehensibly complex universe to a comprehensible and, as Nietzsche put it, "concentrated picture . . . [an] abbreviature of phenomena".[37] As such, it is reductive. There are, of course, limits to how much of reality, that "monster of energy . . . a sea of forces flowing and rushing together, eternally changing, eternally flooding back . . . " can be captured by a myth or a world.[38] There is always more outside of the limits of language, the limits of a world, the limits of a tradition, and that more can flood over those limits and reveal them as artificial. As we increasingly hop from world to world throughout our day and throughout our lives, each world is made increasingly fragile. Good worlds—worlds that contribute to human flourishing—become fragile and no longer compel.

A good world, then, needs protection from the onslaught of the new, or it will become another ephemeral and consumable form of entertainment. Not only does the onslaught of the new threaten current good worlds, but it threatens the possibility of future good worlds. The revolution Arendt longs for has no safe place to come into existence.

Scholars that devote their lives to academic production, often think that they are doing something morally good. They are ostensibly increasing the amount of knowledge and increasing our understanding of the universe. But as Arendt points out in a discussion of scientific discovery, often what scientists discover is not knowledge that is comprehensible to the layman, but knowledge that is so steeped in mathematical and/or specialized language that it is incommunicable to the layman. It boggles common sense.

Arendt used the phrase "common sense" to describe the basic shared understanding of the participants in a particular world. The onslaught of the new can overwhelm common sense, fragmenting it and proliferating worlds. Each of the new worlds will have its own common sense, but these common senses are not necessarily communicable. The result of the onslaught of the new, then, may indeed be new knowledge, but it may very well break or destroy old knowledge.

Scholars like to think that what they are doing is adding pieces to the growing body of knowledge, but from the perspective of a necessarily limited particular world, this is more like junk being added to a mountain of suffocating junk.

The metaphors we use to articulate what is happening in academic production are very telling in this regard. As we will see in Chapter 5, academic production has historically often been conceived as building an edifice, arranging pieces of a puzzle, or mapping reality, but Borges might suggest it is adding another book to the endless library full of gibberish.

The outlook Arendt is articulating is very alien to our modern paradigm of production and our modern desire for abundance. Before turning to these questions, I want to try and use the insights from Nietzsche, Ortega y Gasset, and Arendt to attempt to articulate a theory or model of the consumer cacophony—the supernova proliferation of worlds on the one hand and the stable core of *homo economicus* and the logic of accumulation.

Notes

1. Nietzsche, Friedrich, *The Gay Science* (New York, NY: Cambridge University Press, 2001), 341.

2. Ibid., 276.

3. Ibid., 12.

4. Ibid., aphorism 373.

5. Nietzsche, Friedrich, *The Birth of Tragedy* (New York, NY: Dover, 1995), 85.

6. Nietzsche, Friedrich, *The Will to Power* (New York, NY: Vintage, 1968), 550.

7. Pack, Justin. *Amor Mundi and Overcoming Modern World Alienation* (New York, NY: Lexington Press, 2019).

8. Ibid., 70.

9. Arendt, Hannah. *The Human Condition* (Chicago, IL: University of Chicago Press, 1998), 1.

10 Ibid.

11 Ibid., 2.

12 Ibid., 2–3.

13 Ibid., 6.

14 Ibid., 52

15 Ibid., 197.

16 Basso, Keith H. *Wisdom Sits in Places: Landscape and Language Among the Western Apache* (Albuquerque, NM: University of New Mexico Press, 1996); Pack, Justin. *Amor Mundi and Overcoming Modern World Alienation* (New York, NY: Lexington Press, 2019).

17 Graeber, David and David Wengrow. *The Dawn of Everything: A New History of Humanity* (New York, NY: Farrar, Straus and Giroux, 2021); Pack, Justin. *Prehistoric Philosophy: The Neolithic Revolution, the Indigenous Critique, and the Myths of Civilization* (New York: Bloomsbury Press, forthcoming).

18 Arendt, Hannah. *The Human Condition* (Chicago: University of Chicago Press, 1998), 248.

19 Ibid., 250.

20 Ibid., 250.

21 Jonas, Hans. *The Imperative of Responsibility: In Search of an Ethics of a Technological Age* (Chicago: University of Chicago Press, 1985).

22 Tucker, ed., *The Marx and Engels Reader* (Second Edition) (New York: W.W. Norton & Company, 1978), 432.

23 Arendt, Hannah. *The Human Condition* (Chicago: University of Chicago Press, 1998), 267.

24 Ibid., 4.

25 Ibid., 280.

26 Ibid., 283.

27 Arendt, Hannah. "Culture and Politics." In *Reflections on Literature and Culture*, edited by Susannah Young-ah Gottlieb (Stanford, CA: Stanford University Press, 2007), 179–200.

28 Arendt, Hannah. *The Human Condition* (Chicago: University of Chicago Press, 1998), 126.

29 Young, Julian. *The Death of God and the Meaning of Life* (New York, NY: Routledge, 2003), 208.

30 Levinas, Emmanuel. *Totality and Infinity* (Pittsburgh, PA: Duquesne University Press, 2003).

31 Caputo, John D. *What Would Jesus Deconstruct: The Good News of Postmodernism for the Church* (Ada, MI: Baker Books, 2007).

32 Giddens, Anthony. *The Consequences of Modernity* (Stanford: Stanford University Press, 1991).

33 Arendt, Hannah. *The Human Condition* (Chicago: University of Chicago Press, 1998), 322.

34 Arendt, Hannah. *Between Past and Future* (New York: Penguin Classics, 2006), 186.

35 Pack, Justin. "The Need for an Ethics of Sustainable Knowledge Production." *Metaphilosophy* vol. 50, no. 4 (July, 2019), 551–62

36 Pack, Justin. "Is it Morally Wrong to Publish?" In *Philosophical Interventions in Neoliberal Higher Education* (Lexington Press, forthcoming).

37 Nietzsche, Friedrich, *The Birth of Tragedy* (New York, NY: Dover, 1995), 85.

38 Nietzsche, Friedrich, *The Will to Power* (New York, NY: Vintage, 1968), 550.

4
The Dual Structure of Cacophonous Capitalism

Look at the following quote:

Everyday we're bombarded by choices. We need to make instant decisions. We are in endless combat with our own environment, with all its' pace and variety, its' choice and over-choice. What do we buy? Where do we go? What should we think? The make, the model the price, the pitchmen's pleas. Buy now! Keep up with the latest! Don't fall behind! The pre-cooked, pre-packaged, plastic-wrapped, instant society. We're forced to make so many choices, so many decisions. We have to make them quickly. None of us can escape the pressures...

Don't fall behind! Keep up with the latest! Buy now! Technology feeds on knowledge and knowledge expands at a phenomenal rate. Throughout the world, more than a 1,000 books are published everyday, over 30,000 a month, 365,000 a year. A chemistry professor recently stated that he couldn't pass today's examinations because at lease 2/3 of the questions require knowledge that didn't even exist when he graduated . . . This machine makes our lives move fast. Computers combine facts to make new knowledge at such high speed that we cannot absorb it . . .

In the past, art was created for permanence. Today: instant art, fast, computer created, combinations which are created for the moment, beautiful. As old knowledge is replaced by new, and the pace of change accelerates, the young among us know of no other world. Today's little girl is learning a fundamental lesson: man's relation to things is increasingly temporary.[1]

This is from the 1972 documentary *Future Shock*, which is based on Alvin Toffler's bestselling book of the same name. Amusingly, it is narrated by Orson Welles and, since it is fifty years old, it has dated imagery, odd aesthetics, and some wonky language. This makes it all too easy to dismiss, but many of the ideas expressed in this quote are right in line with the concerns made by the authors we have been examining: the accelerating proliferation of information, the onslaught of the new, the rejection of permanence for abundance, the confusion of the resulting cacophony, the fragilization and commodification of our worlds, the loss of instincts.

The book *Future Shock* sold six million copies. At the time, it was a phenomenon. Despite this, as it would have predicted about itself, it has been largely forgotten in the onslaught of the new.

What interests me here is that the concerns raised by Nietzsche, Ortega y Gasset, and Arendt are not unknown—both to academics but also to the general public: fifty years ago, these concerns were trumpeted far and wide. Why has nothing changed?

This question is particularly vexing in light of the ongoing environmental crisis. The problem is rapidly escalating, the science is clear, and yet nothing changes. The Guardian recently published an article with the title "Hopeless and Broken: Why the World's Top Scientists Are in Despair" in which they interviewed 380 climate scientists about the future.[2] They found, as indicated by the title, that these scientists are deeply alarmed by the failure to take the environmental crisis seriously and do anything about it. One scientist states: "I feel resigned to disaster as we cannot separate our love of bigger, better, faster, more, from what will help the greatest number of people survive and thrive. Capitalism has trained us well." Another: "We live in an age of fools." The escalating problem can also be seen in warnings from the IPCC (Intergovernmental Panel on Climate Change), which have gotten more dire with each new report.

While scientists know far more about the depths of these problems than they did fifty years ago, environmentalists were already sounding the alarm about excessive production and consumption when *Future Shock* was published. When I went to elementary school in the 1980s, we were taught to reduce, reuse, and recycle. Of course, this was lipstick on a pig, because the overwhelming message of modern society is produce, produce, and consume.

This is especially clear when we understand both historically and currently how much effort has been and continues to be poured into (re)creating humankind in the image of *homo economicus*—first as a producer, and then as a consumer. Against this overwhelming and ever ongoing interpellation of ourselves as producers and consumers, the calls to reduce, reuse, and recycle are practically meaningless.

I started out writing this chapter with the goal to further articulate the dual structure of cacophonous capitalism, but in the course of doing so, it became clear that I was working on different levels: on one level metaphorically, on another in terms of identity, and yet on a third level in terms of logics. On the one hand, my primary purpose is to distinguish metaphorically between the supernova explosion of information and possibilities and the stable core and its related animating logic(s) that drives the nova effect. But, as you can see by the end of the previous sentence, I have to introduce the idea of a particular logic(s) that drives the nova effect. To clarify this logic(s), I found myself introducing questions of identity: specifically, what I addressed above as the historical and ongoing creation of *homo economicus*. Ultimately, I want to show how the stable core of cacophonous capitalism functions ideologically as the solid ground we can supposedly stand on, which allows for the misguided dismissal of concerns about cacophony. This stable core is a particular kind of world (the abstract world of money) related to a particular identity (*homo economicus*), and certain logics (production, accumulation, consumption, transgression). Since these are all related, it is difficult to talk about one without talking about another. To try and keep my analysis clear, however, I will begin with the metaphorical dual structure of cacophonous capitalism. As we proceed, to help explain this, I will have to add the questions of identity. Then, in the next chapter, I will explicitly address the different logics at work here.

The Nova Effect

Metaphors are particularly important to the analysis I am offering. Nietzsche describes reality as a vast "sea of forces" and myth as a "maternal" safe place from the fundamental turbulence of reality. Ortega y Gasset speaks of the *"selva selvaggia"*—a suffocating jungle that overwhelms us. Arendt invokes the "onslaught of the new," the brainless animality of labor, and of "human bodies gradually . . . covered by shell of steel" (her metaphor for the reduction of humanity to Kafkaesque machines).[3]

In the introduction, I quoted Charles Taylor's comparison of the medieval city with the modern city. The medieval city is organized around a cathedral which, of course, reflects the organization of a world around religious beliefs. But the modern city no longer has one clear central organizing feature. Architecturally, the "modern metropolis" is full of all sorts of buildings and monuments; "vast areas of city form a crazy quilt of special purpose constructions—factories, malls, docks—following each some fragmented instrumental rationality . . . " There is no longer any clear central organizing structure. This reflects "cacophony replacing meaning as such."[4] This metaphor of a loud, noisy, fragmented modern city does a good job of capturing the multiple logics and complex social and moral tensions in the modern world.

Complaints about the chaos of modern life are not new. One of the most powerful counterclaims to accusations of modern chaos is Adam Smith's well-known image of the "invisible hand" of the market. While Smith himself only used the phrase three times in all his works, the metaphor has taken on a life of its own and has come to have a strange quasi-divine status: although the massive increase of people, products, buildings, possibilities, and worlds in modernity may look chaotic and overwhelming, there is nonetheless a logic to all this, and we can understand it through the study of economics.

In a role oddly similar to the traditional Western understanding of God, the invisible hand explains why things happen the way they do. Metaphorically, it both stands behind the chaos but also suffuses it as the logic that drives these changes. While the logic of the invisible hand doesn't guarantee everything turns out the way we might like, it does offer a supposedly consistent and coherent logic animating all these changes. It doesn't offer the same kind of salvation, but it does reveal at the center of all this a common human nature (*homo economicus*), a common rationality (calculative rationality), and a vision of justice (meritocracy).

What we need then is a metaphor that includes both the chaotic, explosive, and proliferating qualities critics worry about, but also finds a way to include the supposed rationality underlying all the madness. One potential metaphor is a hurricane or a maelstrom, which includes both an expanding and destructive chaos, but also the safety of the eye of the storm or the organizing center of a maelstrom. This does capture the experience of chaos, but it doesn't do enough to capture the explosion and acceleration in modernity. Taylor calls this the "nova effect."[5] Following his lead, this is the metaphor that I think best models the dual aspects of cacophonous capitalism: the exploding supernova and the orienting "energy" or logic that suffuses this process and can supposedly be articulated, thus providing us a reason for what is happening and potentially a feeling of safety through the semi-divine invisible hand.

The metaphor of a supernova is also desirable because both sides, the advocates and the critics, will find it useful to describe what they like or what concerns them. Let me explain. Modernity has often been described as looking forward and premodernity as looking backward.

The project of modernity is actively imagining new possibilities and seeking to remake the present in light of these future possibilities. Premodernity, on the other hand, looks backward to the past, to the founders, the great books, the historical dynasties, and truths that we have forgotten and need to recover and emulate. An underappreciated part of this shift is a difference in attitude toward "more." Hunter-gatherers were content with enough.[6] With the rise of coinage and money in the ancient world came mounting criticisms of the endless addiction to more, which Aristotle called *pleonexia*. Axial texts are full of warnings against excessive desire for more and methods for resisting it (Stoicism, Epicureanism, Cynicism, Daoism, Buddhism, etc.). There was a deep suspicion of money and the ways the desire for more would undermine the ability to have peace, *ataraxia*.[7] In many ways, and with regard to more, modernity breaks with these traditional concerns and, as Arendt argues, embraces abundance and the logic of accumulation. Instead of being critical of too much, modernity is unique in that it embraces the supernova. For modern advocates of the logic of accumulation, the metaphor of a supernova evokes new possibilities, freedom, and a brighter future. For critics, it evokes confusion, onslaught, and suffocation.

A New Myth, a New Religion?

There is a lot of overlap between some of the terminology we have been looking at. For example, "myth" for Nietzsche is very much like what we normally think of when we speak of myths: stories and narratives, often fantastic, that are central to a particular tradition and the identity of those who live in that tradition. A myth both shapes and embodies a world. Thus, when Nietzsche discusses myths, he is also discussing worlds, meaning, and morality. A myth might also demonstrate a particular logic, that is, a particular way of thinking and acting. These sorts of questions are not only the concern of philosophy but also religion. Often when people think of religion, they think of gods and the worship of those gods, but there are religions without gods (Confucianism and Daoism are often academically understood this way). In a strictly sociological sense, a religion is a way of organizing a people and endowing them with a tradition that gives them a sense of purpose and identity. Using this sort of definition, Julian Young has argued that we can and should think of Nietzsche as a philosopher of religion.[8]

In this sense, consumer capitalism is a religion. It is, in its way, a moral order with a new spirituality guided by the myth of the invisible hand and a politics of meritocracy that sanctifies the logic of accumulation and disciplined calculative rationality—altogether the world of *homo economicus*. These terms can shift around in ways that can help us better understand this world. For example, we could speak of the myth of *homo economicus* and the world of the invisible hand. We could also describe this brave new world as a world of money: abstract money people, calculative, and quantitative money thought, accumulation-driven money dreams.

While secular capitalist modernity is not normally articulated as a religion, critics have argued that it often acts like one.[9] Harvey Cox, a religious scholar, was alerted to this when he noticed how much the language in the business section of the New York Times reminded him of theological language:

Instead I was surprised to discover that most of the concepts I ran across were strangely familiar. Expecting terra incognita, I found myself instead in the land of déjà vu. The lexicon of the *Wall Street Journal*, *Financial Times*, and the *Economist* turned out to bear a striking resemblance to Genesis, the Epistle to the Romans, and Saint Augustine's City of God. Behind descriptions of acquisitions and mergers, monetary policy, and the convolutions of the Dow and the NASDAQ, I gradually made out the pieces of a grand narrative about the inner meaning of human history, why things go wrong, and how to put them right. Theologians call these myths of origin, legends of the fall and doctrines of sin and redemption. Here they were again, and in only thin disguise: chronicles about the creation of wealth, the seductive temptations of over-regulation, captivity to faceless business cycles, and, ultimately, salvation through the advent of free markets, with a small dose of ascetic belt-tightening along the way for those economies that fall into the sin of arrears. I realized then that my many years of studying religion and theology had prepared me to approach this mysterious thing called the economy more knowingly than I could have guessed.[10]

Boldeman offers a very critical picture of economists as the priests of a new cult. He is worth quoting at length:

[E]conomics threatens to become the dominant rationalist and fundamentalist religion of contemporary capitalist society and of the emerging global civilization. This threat is aided by its attempt to appropriate the prestige associated with the natural sciences. Importantly, it is easy to slip between the uses of individualism as an analytical tool to a promotion of individualism as a normative ideal. This religion is of particular appeal to business and political elites because it tends to legitimize greed, love of money and power. It is leading to the commercialization of all human activity, while aiding the atomization and privatization of competing values and groups. It has elevated money beyond a convenience to the means of salvation and the source of meaning, values and security, turning it, and the mechanism for acquiring it, into idols.

Economists—the prophets and priests of this new religion—preach about and have a major impact on public policy and our institutional arrangements. Economics therefore provides an alternative faith tradition, complete with values, ideas of welfare and of progress—usually defined in terms of quantitative economic indicators, which dominate public discourse and which seek to reshape our institutions and organizations. With their influence on government, economists are the new theocracy, the contemporary manifestation of Plato's guardians. In particular, the economic theologian's rhetoric resembles contemporary process theology. In this school, although God will possess the classic attributes of omnipotence (all power), omniscience (all knowledge) and omnipresence (present everywhere), He does not yet possess them in full. Such a theology offers considerable comfort to the economic theologian, explaining the dislocation, pain and disorientation that are the results of transitions from economic heterodoxy to free markets. THE MARKET is becoming more like Yahweh of the Old Testament: not just one superior deity contending with others, but the Supreme Deity, the only true God, whose reign must now be accepted universally and who allows no rivals. There is no conceivable limit to THE MARKET's inexorable ability to convert creation into commodities. In the church of THE MARKET, everything—no matter how sacred—eventually becomes a commodity. This radical de-sacralizing dramatically alters the human relationship to land, water, air and space. Indeed, human beings themselves start to become commodities as well.... THE MARKET has become the most formidable rival to traditional religions, not least because it is rarely recognized as a religion. The contradictions between the world-views of traditional religion and the world-view of THE MARKET religion are so basic that no compromise seems possible.[11]

While I am sympathetic to the critique being offered here, it is not my primary purpose in quoting this passage. What is important here is the point that a discipline, economics, can come to function like a religion. It provides myths, it promises salvation, it offers an explanation for why things happen, it claims epistemic authority which in turn supports a political project, it offers a particular rationality, it offers an uncompromising and therefore powerful "world-view" or, as Arendt would say, world. When speaking of this world, we could follow Boldeman in speaking of an economic world, but I will more often refer to consumer capitalism or neoliberalism since these are broader terms that capture more of what is happening in this world.

Boldeman describes economics as a jealous god that will tolerate no rivals. This may be true at the level of intellectual debate and contemporary politics, but in many ways consumer capitalism is quite the opposite: it seemingly tolerates anything and everything. All other worlds, while ostensibly rivals, are potential sources of profit and can be commodified and subsumed under the umbrella of neoliberal freedom. Buddhism: commodifiable. Buy your Buddha statue here. Indigenous traditions: commodifiable. Dreamcatchers for sale. Environmentalism: commodifiable. New environmentally friendly soaps have arrived. Communism: commodifiable. Che Guevara shirts available! Boldeman is right that there is a critical danger here, but it is not only because of the intellectual and political hegemony of neoliberalism, but also because of the way it encourages the proliferation of worlds while simultaneously promising that the invisible hand will keep us safe.

This is precisely what makes consumer capitalism so different from previous worlds. While other worlds would be concerned about the cacophony and confusion of too much, neoliberalism encourages and embraces the nova effect: more worlds mean more money. The collapse of one world means those who dwelt in that world will have to move into another and buy what that world offers. Fragmentation and proliferation drive profits. While they may be painful to those losing their gods, there are ever more products to fill God-shaped holes.

To understand the dual structure of cacophonous capitalism, we need to understand something of the world of *homo economicus* and logic of accumulation that drives the nova effect. Let's turn to this now.

Homo Economicus: A Money World

The term *homo economicus* describes a type of human or a type of human behavior. It is a new type of human—likely unique to modernity. Humans in the past were concerned with many things, but the economic was always less a concern than the social.[12] Even when humans enslaved other humans, it was not economic gain that was their goal but honor and power.[13] The economic goal of accumulation is a relatively new and relatively odd aim. Aristotle famously argued that humans want happiness and that there are different ways to accomplish that happiness, but that we need to be careful mistaking means for ends. Money can be helpful to get happiness, for example by giving us free time to be with friends and family (the sort of thing Aristotle thinks will bring us the most happiness) or participate as citizens in the *polis*, but some people make the mistake of thinking money is an end-in-itself and end up caught in an endless quest for more and more money. Sadly, they can miss the best things in life because they are addicted to accumulating money, which Aristotle calls *pleonexia*.

Homo economicus does not refer to people addicted to money, but to a type of human who thinks and acts in the ways described by neoclassical economists. *Homo economicus* is constantly calculating and acting so as to maximize his or her preferences and minimize the costs of accomplishing desired benefits. It can be a very entrepreneurial approach to life, but also just a very utilitarian one. Since every person has different preferences, what every *homo economicus* seeks will be different, but they will tend to seek their goals with an eye to efficiency and with a constant cost/benefit analysis. Money, since it is exchangeable for many things, is highly desirable as something that enables accomplishing or obtaining the various goals of *homo economicus*.

Initially, *homo economicus* was articulated as an ideal. Considering how much Aristotle and much of the ancient world warned against this, it is a striking historical development.[14] Why would some modern thinkers embrace the ideal of *homo economicus*? One reason, as Albert Hirschman has argued, is that *homo economicus* is relatively predictable.[15] If everyone acted like *homo economicus*, it would allow us to predict human behavior with much more accuracy than has been possible previously. Humans do all sorts of things for all sorts of reasons, but if they all acted similarly, we could anticipate and manage that behavior much more easily. But why not idealize and standardize a more . . . moral kind of behavior? Two reasons. First, it was claimed, it is easier to get people to act in their self-interest than in more altruistic ways. Second, despite there being vices, self-interested behaviors could be highly productive. People will work harder if they get more of what they want for doing so.

All of these claims have been contested, both on moral grounds and based on evidence from social scientists and economists.[16] Despite this, recently, coinciding with the rise of neoliberalism, there has been a push from some economists, most famously Gary Becker, not only for the *ideal* of *homo economicus*, but for the claim that human nature is *homo economicus*. This is not the claim that we should be, but the claim that we already are *homo economicus*. This means that when we do something that seems altruistic, there must actually must be ulterior self-interested motives. Even though the evidence does not indicate humans think or act naturally in this manner, this approach pushes *homo economicus* under the surface, so that at bottom, everything is rational choice theory. There are, of course, many criticisms of this approach also.[17]

Why, if there is not strong evidence that *homo economicus* is a good description of human behavior, nor compelling reasons to take it at face value as a good ideal, has this image had such influence in modernity? We will look at two reasons here. First, while *homo economicus* is in many ways (certainly from most, if not all, traditional premodern perspectives[18]) morally distasteful, it has proven powerful as a part of a larger ideal: meritocracy. Second, it was forced on people against their will—in other words a major part of the project of modernity was to reshape humankind in the image of *homo economicus*. Let's look at each of these claims in turn.

Meritocracy

Homo economicus is not a very attractive ideal. But meritocracy, on the other hand, has proven to be a powerful ideal that makes *homo economicus* look much more attractive than it does without it. What then is meritocracy?

The ideal of meritocracy is not new. It is present in Confucianism and some other ancient traditions. The basic idea is that those who are put in positions of power should earn those positions through merit and not, as in an aristocracy, through birth. A meritocratic system seeks to find those that can produce the best results. In the United States currently, this is often reduced to the more doubtful claim that hard work leads to success.

The claim that hard work leads to success is often known as the American Dream, which says that if you work hard, you will be able to afford a house with a white picket fence and many of the other benefits of consumer capitalism. Even though this claim is clearly false since many people do work hard but do not accomplish these things, the image of the American Dream is held onto very tightly by many Americans. Not only this, the fallacious inverse that those who are not successful must not have worked is also unfortunately often held to be true.

The reason these false claims are held onto so tightly despite being so misguided is because meritocracy functions like a theology—by which I mean it makes sense of the evils and inequalities of this world. Since everyone can succeed if they try, everyone deserves what they have. If a particular family is rich, they must have worked hard for it. If another family is poor, they need to work harder, and then they too can be rich.

This outlook excuses the rich from having to care for the poor. After all, if they worked hard, they could be rich too. It also justifies the rich in having larger houses, nicer cars, better clothes, and so on— again, everyone can have these things if they try. In fact, any kind of government intervention to redistribute wealth from the wealthy to the poor is terribly unjust. Not only does it take from those who have earned it, but it takes away the motivation to work from those who are poor.

In a previous book, I examined how meritocratic explanations have been adopted in many conservative Christian churches in the United States and how traditional Christian values of grace, helping the poor, and social justice are being replaced by meritocratic ideals of work, riches, and justified inequality.[19] One of the more disturbing aspects of this change is how meritocracy claims to offer justice in this world—to the hard workers, wealth, and to the lazy, poverty—and, by doing so, undercuts the traditional Christian vision of justice in the next life. In other words, meritocracy offers justice now instead of the delayed justice traditionally offered by Christianity in the next life. The God who offers righteous judgment in the next life is replaced by a god that offers justice (through inequality) now.

The promises of this-worldly salvation are open to those who think and act like *homo economicus*. Those who don't maximize their portfolio will be left behind in the merited hell of poverty.

Changing Human Nature

I remember taking an economic history class as an undergraduate and the professor explaining things like the movement (and proletarianization) of English peasant farmers to the industrial factories by saying that they "voted with their feet." This struck me as quite odd at the time, since I had just read Karl Polanyi's *The Great Transformation* in a sociology course, and Polanyi had shown how the peasants were forced off the land through various enclosure movements. Government requirements that the peasantry fence in their land basically forced them to sell their land and move into the cities.[20] Here was the same event presented as a movement of freedom in economics and as a brutal act of proletarianization in sociology.

Silvia Federici has offered a harrowing counternarrative to the "voted with their feet" narrative of modern progress.[21] Building on Foucault, she argues there was a concerted effort to force the peasants off their farms and into the factories. This involved not just the political acts of expropriation but a radical shift in human nature and self-understanding. The mechanical philosophy of Descartes and Hobbes changed how humans related to the physical world, but also how they related to themselves. Unlike the enchanted cosmos, which required personal relationships, the mechanical world required human intervention to "improve" it.[22] Since human bodies are also mechanical, they too could be improved through proper control—mind over matter. Proletariats were increasingly expected to think about themselves this way and to act accordingly. Their bodies were useful, their labor was useful, but it had to be controlled and used by a disciplined mind. What Federici claims is that proletariat bodies were increasingly treated as potentially valuable commodities that needed to be managed by others and by their own minds if possible.

Federici is not alone in tracing this shift. Many other scholars, most famously Foucault, have also seen the disciplinary project as an important part of modernity.[23] For our purposes here, what Federici shows is that the calculative and disciplinary approach of *homo economicus* toward the world and themselves is not natural at all, but a product of the project of modernity.

The World of Money and Trust

Of course, the efforts to remake humankind in the image of *homo economicus* were not limited to humans but extended to remaking the world(s) itself. While this project is ongoing (each new generation of humans needs to be "educated" and shaped into producers and consumers), once our institutions and practices have been suffused with the utilitarian and calculative logic of production, accumulation, and consumption they tend to reproduce themselves.

There are obviously many ways to describe our modern world, but perhaps the most straightforward would be to call it a world of money. I don't think this claim is controversial. Especially with the rise of neoliberalism after Thatcher and Reagan, money and the logic of efficiency have been spreading further throughout modern institutions. "Market triumphalism" shows no signs of slowing.[24]

While the world of money is a world of fragmentation and cacophony, it is also a world of trust. This would have seemed completely counterintuitive to most premodern peoples, for whom money was viewed with deep mistrust and from whom a world of money would have been viewed as a world of mistrust.[25] But the social theorist Anthony Giddens argues that the modern world (of money) actually requires a lot of trust, albeit a different kind of trust than the face-to-face trust of a small community. Drawing on Goffman, he argues living in cities with many strangers requires "civil inattention."[26] This means we don't treat strangers with suspicion and instead understand that there are many strangers in the world around us who make the things we eat, wear, drive, and so on, and that we are all part of an interconnected web in which we all affect each other in various ways that we have little control over—and as such we can ignore strangers and not worry about them. We have to trust that they, like us, will do their part—or that if they don't, they will be replaced by someone else that will. This implies a trust in the "abstract systems" that function like the machinery of modern society. Furthermore, this implies a trust in the expertise of others that keeps this machinery functioning.

While this is nothing like the trust of face-to-face relationships, it is still clearly a kind of trust. We see this kind of trust with money itself.

Money is an abstract object that, to function, requires trust. If people don't trust their government or a particular form of money enough, they will not use government-created coinage or money. They will instead use IOUs, credit, and other forms of tracking exchanges.[27] Alternatively, high inflation can undermine trust in a particular currency and can lead to people in some countries using the currency of a different one. The point I am trying to make is that it takes trust to assume that a stranger will give you food for a piece of paper or some coins. The world of money has its own kind of trust.

The different forms of trust that Giddens points to are interrelated and buttress each other. Expertise reinforces faith in abstract systems. Functioning abstract systems reinforce expectations that others will act according to the rules. The behavior of these strangers matches my own closely enough. Furthermore, as we saw earlier, the world of *homo economicus*, especially when bolstered by meritocratic ideals, functions like a religion. It offers worldly salvation through the American Dream and turns a world of inequality into a just order. If narratives and ethics like this are sufficiently widespread, then, despite the ways the imperatives of production and accumulation lead to fragmentation and cacophony, there is always the anchor world amids the supernova effect.

The Dual Structure of Cacophonous Capitalism

It is in this sense that even if there is a proliferating cacophony of worlds, there is a constant world underlying everything else. This is what I mean by the dual structure of cacophonous capitalism: as confusing and disorienting as the cacophony may be, there is safety in the eye of the storm—the world of money.

Calling the world of money the "safety in the eye of the storm" is a useful metaphor to see why some do not feel lost in the proliferation of worlds—they can find meaning playing the game of meritocracy or moral order in the ideals of *homo economicus*. It is this kind of metaphor that has resulted in me speaking of a stable "core" of modernity at various points so far. The problem with the metaphor of a hurricane is that it separates the stable core from the chaotic storm. The advantage of the metaphor of a supernova explosion is that it captures the chaos and proliferation but also is expanding and spreading. There is an energy that suffuses and drives the expansion. Metaphorically, this energy is the "logics" of production, accumulation, consumption, and transgression. These logics drive the supernova explosion forward. They push for more.

So instead of a stable core, I think it likely makes more sense to speak of logics that animate the supernova. The logics are obviously related to the world of money and *homo economicus*, but they are diffuse instead of a kind of core. I will try to further articulate these logics in the next chapter.

It may not be entirely apparent at this point why I am seeking to articulate the dual structure of cacophonous capitalism. On the one hand, as I have been attempting to show in this chapter, not everyone feels the loss that Nietzsche and Arendt describe, nor the feeling of suffocation of Ortega y Gasset's *selva selvaggia*. The dual structure helps explain how we can have both the fragmentation and proliferation of worlds and yet simultaneously a secure world (of money). Stated alternatively, we have a mad profusion of worlds and logics, and yet a set of consistent logics (produce, consume, accumulate) that tend to run throughout the rest. The stable logics and the "core" world of money function to drive the proliferation of worlds and consumer cacophony while simultaneously assuring us that all is well. There is a reason for all of this.

A careful reader will note that I have included and omitted a fourth logic (transgression) at various points. The first three logics (produce, consume, accumulate) are clearly related to capitalism. The logic of transgression can play an active role in capitalism, but it does not always.

My interest in the logic of transgression has to do with its role in academia, specifically in the humanities. And my interest in academia with regards to cacophony concerns the failure of academics to work through these issues. Academics are supposedly thoughtful. But if that is the case, why is there so little thinking about cacophony and so little resistance to it?

Traditionally, academia functions differently from capitalism, but in the last fifty years, universities have been increasingly neoliberalized.[28] This has created interesting tensions, especially with regard to academic production.

The situation is complicated because during roughly the same time, academics in the humanities have become increasingly concerned with the ways that knowledge has been used to colonize and standardize human populations (both internally and externally), destroying traditional cultures and turning everyone into *homo economicus*. Furthermore, there has been an increased concern with marginalized groups and marginalized knowledge. One of the results of these concerns is the embrace of a logic of transgression that seeks to challenge, break, and transgress the categories, boundaries, and limitations of the project of modernity.

The problem is that the logic of transgression is often appropriated and used by consumer capitalism. For example, the transgression of heteronormativity by a pop singer may succeed to some degree in challenging homophobic norms, but it may also be leveraged as yet another product to sell by capitalists. Under conditions of proliferation and cacophony, transgression too often becomes another thing to sell.

Between the neoliberalization of academic production and the logic of transgression, academia seems to be increasingly subsumed into consumer capitalism. Rather than breaking with the system, most academics seem to be sucked up into it. But it is not clear that academics understand this or know how to stop it. This indicates the insidious power of cacophonous capitalism.

The next chapter will seek to clarify this conundrum with the help of the social thinker Zygmunt Bauman.

Notes

1 *Future Shock*, 1972.

2 https://www.theguardian.com/environment/ng-interactive/2024/may/08/hopeless-and-broken-why-the-worlds-top-climate-scientists-are-in-despair. Accessed May 14, 2024.

3 Arendt, Hannah. *The Human Condition* (Chicago: University of Chicago Press, 1998), 323.

4 Taylor, Charles. *A Secular Age* (Cambridge, MA: Harvard University Press, 2007), 552.

5 Ibid.

6 Sahlins, Marshall. *Stone Age Economics* (Chicago, IL: Aldine, 1994).

7 Pack, Justin. *Money and Thoughtlessness: A Genealogy and Defense of Traditions Suspicions of Money and Merchants* (New York, NY: Palgrave Macmillan, 2023).

8 Young, Julian. *Nietzsche's Philosophy of Religion* (New York, NY: Cambridge University Press, 2006).

9 Cox, Harvey. *The Market as God* (Cambridge, MA: Harvard University Press, 2016), Boldeman, Lee. *The Cult of the Market: Economic Fundamentalism and its Discontents* (Canberra, Australia: ANU E Press, 2011), McCarraher, Eugene. *The Enchantments of Mammon: How Capitalism became the Religion of Modernity* (Cambridge, MA: Belknap Press, 2019).

10 Cox, Harvey. *The Market as God* (Cambridge, MA: Harvard University Press, 2016).

11 Boldeman, Lee. *The Cult of the Market: Economic Fundamentalism and its Discontents* (Canberra, Australia: ANU E Press, 2011), 278–9.

12 Graeber, David. *Debt: The First 5,000 Years* (Brooklyn, NY: Melville House, 2014).

13 Patterson, Orlando. *Slavery and Social Death* (Cambridge, MA: Harvard University Press, 2018).

14 Pack, Justin. *Money and Thoughtlessness: A Genealogy and Defense of Traditions Suspicions of Money and Merchants* (New York, NY: Palgrave Macmillan, 2023).

15 Hirshman, Albert. *The Passions and the Interests: Political Arguments for Capitalism before Its Triumph* (Princeton, NJ: Princeton University Press, 1977).

16 There are many examples of criticisms that could be cited. The recent *Cathonomics* compiles many of these concerns. Annett, Anthony M. *Cathonomics: How Catholic Tradition Can Create a More Just Economy* (Washington DC: Georgetown University Press, 2022).

17 See for example, Sandel, Michael. *What Money Can't Buy: The Moral Limits of Markets* (New York, NY: Farrar, Straus and Giroux, 2013).

18 Pack, Justin. *Money and Thoughtlessness: A Genealogy and Defense of Traditions Suspicions of Money and Merchants* (New York, NY: Palgrave Macmillan, 2023).

19 Pack, Justin. *Meritocracy Mingled with Scripture* (By Common Consent Press, 2024).

20 Polanyi, Karl. *The Great Transformation: The Political and Economic Origins of Our Time* (Boston, MA: Beacon Press, 2001).

21 Federici, Silvia. *Caliban and the Witch: Women, the Body and Primitive Accumulation* (New York, NY: Autonomedia, 2004).

22 Merchant, Carolyn. *The Death of Nature: Women Ecology and the Scientific Revolution* (New York: Harper and Row, 1990).

23 Foucault, Michel. *Discipline and Punish* (New York: NY: Vintage Books, 1995); Taylor, Charles. *Sources of the Self: The Making of Modern Identity* (Boston, MA: Harvard University Press, 1992).

24 Sandel, Michael. *What Money Can't Buy: The Moral Limits of Markets* (New York, NY: Farrar, Straus and Giroux, 2013).

25 Pack, Justin. *Money and Thoughtlessness: A Genealogy and Defense of Traditions Suspicions of Money and Merchants* (New York, NY: Palgrave Macmillan, 2023).

26 Giddens, Anthony. *The Consequences of Modernity* (Stanford, CA: Stanford University Press, 1991), 81.

27 This is what was done in rural New England. See Clark, Christopher. *The Roots of Rural Capitalism: Western Massachusetts 1780–1860* (Ithica, NY: Cornell University Press, 1992).

28 Pack, Justin. *How the Neoliberalization of Academia Leads to Thoughtlessness: Arendt and the Modern University* (New York: Lexington Books, 2018).

5

Production and Transgression in Liquid Modernity

In the last chapter, I attempted to flesh out the dual structure of cacophonous capitalism. In this chapter, I want to explore the logics that drive and suffuse the supernova explosion. These include production, accumulation, consumption, and transgression.

By "logic" I mean the ideas, reasons, and actions that are associated with a particular practice and give it coherency. In this sense, many activities have their own logics. Thus, there is a logic to playing American football, to giving a presentation at a biology conference, to writing a book. For those who do not know how to do those things, the "logic" of these activities may not be clear. But once one becomes conversant in the "language" of a particular game or activity, there is a logic that begins to make sense. American football is infamous for some of its weird rules, but once you understand them, you begin to see that there are games within a game based on how one responds to the various logics at play.

As I explained at the end of the last chapter, I am interested in how some of these logics play out in academia. I have three reasons for this. First, because it seems to me that academics should be one of the groups most concerned about the problem of cacophony, but alarmingly there is little discussion of it and little done about it. On the contrary, as a result of the neoliberalization of higher education and the rise of the logic of transgression in the humanities, academia is suffused with the logic of production. The second reason for looking at academia specifically is because the logic of production and transgression in academia is more complex than simply making money. Examining this will help us see how the logic of production and transgression is overdetermined: there are multiple similar logics that reinforce each other. Lastly, the third reason for dwelling on academia is because I am inclined to agree with Ortega y Gasset that one of the fundamental missions of the university should be the management of cacophony. I want to encourage moving in this direction.

To help elaborate the argument I want to make, I will use the social theorist Zygmunt Bauman. Bauman will help illustrate the dynamics involved in the logic of transgression in what he originally saw as a shift from modernity to postmodernity and later redescribed as a shift from "solid modernity" to "liquid modernity." These terms are helpful to see changes in the logic of academic production.

I will begin by making a few points about the logic of accumulation and production in early modernity, the addition of the imperative of consumption to the imperative of production at the turn of the twentieth century, and then turn to Bauman to explore later changes.

Accumulation and Production

What is meant by accumulation and production has changed over time. Furthermore, there are also different kinds of accumulation and production that can occur simultaneously. To clarify this, let's briefly look at how accumulation in prehistory was very different from accumulation in modernity. Then, let's look at how there are currently multiple different logics of production.

Our contemporary everyday understandings of accumulation and production tend to be related to money. Generally, accumulation refers to the process of obtaining ever more money (or things), and production refers to making things or performing services in order to get paid money. It should be pointed out that both of these have a penumbra of moral meanings that accompany them. If accumulation is saving money and being frugal, it is often viewed as honorable. If it is being done by a very wealthy individual, it can become curmudgeonly, excessive, and ugly. Being productive is often viewed as morally praiseworthy, but excessive demands to be productive are alienating and exploitative. Generally, as long as a community is committed to something like the Protestant ethic, being productive is seen a virtue. Accumulation, as long as it is reasonable, is virtuous, but if excessive, it can become a vice.

While this is how we understand accumulation and production now and it is what most of us spend our lives doing, it is important to recognize that these money-driven logics of accumulation and production appear very late in human history with the modern creation of *homo economicus*. *Homo sapiens* have traditionally not been motivated by accumulating the abstract thing we call money nor producing things in order to accumulate money. If they were interested in accumulating anything, it was likely to be social recognition (or honor).[1] Such recognition could be achieved through religious rituals, gift ceremonies, competitions, warfare, slavery—in other words, accumulating people (and/or influence on, control over, relationships with, or honor from people).

The accumulation of money appears as a very strange and misguided effort from most premodern perspectives. Among other reasons, this is because with most things there is a limit to how much one can accumulate. You can only accumulate so many personal relationships or so many material possessions. At a certain point, further accumulation becomes unwieldy and cumbersome. The odd thing about abstract money is that it seems it can be accumulated indefinitely. To modern eyes, it is understandable why money is so addicting: it can be exchanged for many other things. But when you combine this with the abstract nature of money, you end up with something that is particularly dangerous, because there is no clear limit to how much money one can acquire. Is there ever too much money? Once the momentum of accumulating gets rolling, it can be hard to slow or stop it. Once we get a taste for money, it is hard to sate our desire for it. This was known by many ancient and medieval philosophers, and they offered many warnings about money and *aura sacra fames*.[2]

Without the frantic demands of the accumulation of insatiable money, production takes on a very different tone. As Weber points out, for most premodern people, the point of life was not to produce, but to play, or engage in ritual, or learn, or worship gods, or one of many other things that gave life meaning.³ Production tended to only be done to produce a certain amount of necessities. Working more than this would only be done if one was forced to.

The last chapter gave us a glimpse into the efforts of scholars to understand the modern project to reshape humans and the world in the image of *homo economicus*. I will not expand on that discussion here. Rather, what I want to do next is look at the logic of production in academia. Originally, under positivism, this was a very different kind of production. Elaborating on how it works will help not only to show how there can be different and often reinforcing logics (in this case the logic of production of goods and the logic of the production of knowledge), but also help us to understand the background to the rise of the logic of transgression.

Academic Production

Academic production is different from economic production. The origin of academic production is the modern research university, which developed in Germany in the late 1800s.⁴ It was shaped by the ideals of positivism. Positivism, first articulated by French thinkers Comte and Saint-Simon, is a version of the project of modernity or the Enlightenment that strongly emphasizes the role of science in establishing the truth and shaping modern society for the better:

> Comte's views can be summarized as five basic principles. (1) Comte sought to adapt the successful methods of the physical sciences for the study of society and to unify all the branches of

science through a common methodology based on empirical observation, comparisons of condition, experimentation, and quantitative calculation. (2) He held that the world consisted of observable, measureable phenomena (facts) and regulative patterns and relationships between phenomena (laws). (3) He rejected the search for ultimate purposes or the underlying nature (or essences) of phenomena as an activity outside the purview of science. (4) He believed that knowledge in all branches of science unfolds in progressive stages, the final stage being positivism. (5) Lastly, Comte argued that the ultimate purpose of science was to promote social progress and order.[5]

Different metaphorical images have been invoked by positivists (and others) to describe the process of academic production. Descartes could be seen as offering the basic image that inspired positivism. He argues in the *Discourse on Method*, that we should break any difficulty into "as many parts as possible" in order to find the basic components, and then systematically work in an "orderly fashion" from simple parts to a larger whole that avoids any omissions.[6] This is a kind of Lego model of knowledge production: take things apart and put them back together.

The German positivist Ranke tried to apply this approach to history by insisting historians only seek "what actually happened" and the "strict presentation of facts."[7] In his vision, historians should focus on "minutiae" and then cobble together the pieces they discover into "a larger context" until a "fullness and totality" of "universal history" is produced.[8] Later positivist historians Bury and Elton used a telling metaphor to describe this process: "Each published piece of research represented a brick and the work of the historian was therefore analogous to that of a skilled craftsman. The analogy is revealing, for neither Bury nor Elton expected, nor desired, the laborer to have knowledge of the larger edifice." Elton thought a good historian should "never raise his eyes beyond the detail of his own minute area of study."[9]

This idea that academic production is like building an edifice brick by brick is a common metaphor, but not the only one. Sometimes academic production is articulated as a map-making endeavor—accurately mapping out new uncharted territories. Each scientist goes out and maps their little part of the world, and when they all report back, we will put all the pieces together to have the map of the whole (Borges made fun of this in his story about a map that matched the world 1:1 and which covered the entire land). Thomas Kuhn argues that scientists are "puzzle solvers," each working on their own piece of the puzzle until the whole is created by fitting all the pieces together.[10]

What is common in the metaphors of brick work, mapping, and puzzle solving is the idea that, as Rorty put it, the obtaining knowledge is a matter of mirroring reality.[11] The key is having the proper method. If we can obtain the right method, as Descartes claimed, we can attain true knowledge—in pieces. And, as Comte taught, with this knowledge we can "promote social progress and order." It is critical to notice the contrast between the seemingly passive act of mirroring and the aggressive active intervention of promoting "social progress and order." First, get the knowledge, then use the knowledge.

Philosophically, positivism has fallen into disrepute, but it continues to exercise a remarkable influence over the moral imaginary and self-understanding of academics. Simply put, the ideals of positivism shaped the creation of the modern research university and are baked into the institution. The very division of academia into disciplines fits with the Cartesian Lego model. Many academics, especially those in the social sciences, continue to see their job as to find knowledge that can be used to inform policymaking and thereby "promote social progress and order." Despite powerful criticisms of positivism, academic production is still suffused with these moral ideals and still understood by most of those involved as critically important social and moral endeavors.

This approach is powerful and has changed the world. Despite this, the question is not only whether it is actually a good theory of how we gain or produce knowledge (it isn't), but also whether, on the one hand, it is imperialist and colonialist and, on the other, whether it is antithetical to the task of managing cacophony.

Zygmunt Bauman offers a striking way of seeing some of the problems here. Bauman describes the project of modernity as a gardening project. When you make a garden, the first step is to make a plan. Then, the area that is to be planted must be cleared and tilled. Whatever existed there before is removed. Then, plants are placed in orderly rows where they will be easy to access and manage. This last point is critical for Bauman. He argues that one of the primary concerns for the gardeners is ambivalence.[12] The world (the garden) has to be divided up into clearly defined rows. If the peas get mixed up with the beans, the crops will be far more difficult to monitor and use.

The metaphor is meant to describe the social engineering pretentions of modernity. As the project of modernity began, Europeans were highly fragmented into different communities with different languages or dialects and different cultural practices. To turn them into *homo economicus*, they had to be relatively homogenized—identities and social commitments had to be shifted from local communities and religion to nations (a process concisely summarized in the title of Eugen Weber's *Peasants into Frenchmen*).[13] Motivations had to be streamlined to primarily emphasize accumulation and production (work).[14] Gender roles were tightened with men increasingly defined as breadwinners and women increasingly defined as home-makers.[15] Sexuality became highly monitored.[16] In short—the great variety of social and cultural practices had to be streamlined and everything had to be placed into its "proper" category or box in order to be managed and monitored accurately and efficiently.

The social engineering performed here is not just done willy nilly. It needs to start with where people are in order to get them to where it wants them to be. This is the side of the problematic that fits with the "mirror of nature" endeavor described by Rorty. Where did the people live? What language did they speak? What were their jobs? James C. Scott does a good job describing the efforts of modern states to make the people of their countries transparent and visible: roads were named, addresses established, names affixed, number of children in the household, farm boundaries, records established, and maintained, a variety of information was gathered through censuses and sometimes imposed (e.g., some people didn't have last names and had to be given them).[17] Just like Descartes' Lego model, the land and people had to be taken apart into its basic components, measured, and weighed—in short quantified, in order to then "fix" them.

This internal colonization was turned outwards as well (or, some argue, began outwards and was applied inwards). While this begins with the discovery of the Americas, the "science"-backed gardening pretentions of modernity are particularly egregious in the colonialism of the 1800s. Europeans took over much of Africa and Asia, surveyed them, and began "fixing"—that is, "modernizing" them to make them profitable. The role of science in this process has been subject to scathing criticism by diverse thinkers, both by those on the colonized side (Said, Fanon, Deloria Jr, etc.) and those on the colonizer side (Foucault, Sartre, Bauman, etc.). Various scientifically informed movements of the 1800s like eugenics and phrenology were used to push racist, sexist, homophobic, and classist social policies. In *Modern and the Holocaust*, Bauman argues that the Nazi efforts to use the best science and most efficient logistical methods to systematically eliminate those deemed "weeds" in the Nazi garden were not an aberration, but an embodiment of modern gardening pretentions.[18]

At one level, these anti-positivist criticisms were aimed at the pretention of objectivity and the alarming ways that the reality that was supposedly mirrored was riven with white supremacy and other crude biases. A common rebuttal to this is that this was not the fault of science, but racist scientists. At a deeper level, however, these criticisms, especially those of Foucault, questioned the separation of knowledge and power, the metaphor of the mirror of nature, and the innocence of quantification.[19] We don't need to delve into these more radical criticisms here to make the point that sadly, not much of this has resulted in significant changes in academic production. Academic work continues to be primarily articulated as mirroring reality and then using that information to inform political policy. The prestige of science (at least within academia) has not diminished, and the typical methods built on the unsophisticated quantification of "reality" remain hegemonic. If anything, these practices are more entrenched than ever.[20] This means that a typical academic will see their primary task as producing more knowledge. In itself, this may not seem unreasonable, but in an endlessly proliferating consumer capitalist society like our own that lacks a corresponding vision and practice of academic, social, and political cacophony management, it only adds to the cacophony.

Bauman argues that this critical problem at the heart of the academic production of knowledge leads to the "revenge of ambivalence."[21] The Lego method of knowledge production is always taking things apart and produces a wild proliferation of pieces of information. But what if reality or the world that we are mirroring is not finite? What if it is like a fractal, and that as you zoom in or out, it changes? Furthermore, what if it is a moving fractal? This is the case for social reality: people are constantly changing, and there is no static, fixed reality we can exhaustively map.

If this is the case, then the attempt to map reality can never finish and will never cease generating new information, new "facts." We could say there are different realities, or different aspects of reality—the reality studied by economics, the reality studied by anthropologists, the reality studied by physicists, and so forth. Would we have to add all these realities together to get some whole? Would the completed maps even fit together? I would suggest that not only would the maps *not* fit together, but the quantum world described by physics should help us see that there is no single reality—or that the different aspects of reality do not add up to a comprehensible whole. Arendt makes the point that the discourses resulting from the hyper-specialization of academic disciplines does not result in clarity, but in the ever-increasing accumulation of facts that are incommunicable from outside of a particular paradigm.[22] In many cases, they cannot even be communicated to the public. The result is ever more knowledge, but knowledge that can only be understood by experts.

The "revenge of ambivalence" is that these new mountains of knowledge do not, in the end, create clarity, but cacophony. Academic production fragments and multiplies realities, and this "fragmentation turns the problem-solving into Sisyphean labour and incapacitates it as a tool of order-making."[23] The irony of all this new knowledge is that is doesn't cohere into a comprehensible whole, but into mazes of incommensurable and even incomprehensible paradigms. "The struggle against ambivalence is, therefore, both self-destructive and self-propelling."[24] The academic production of knowledge initiated by modernity in order to turn the fragmented worlds of premodernity into "solvable little problems" results in a malignant, ever-increasing cacophony.[25]

Consumption

Hopefully the previous discussion has helped show that not only are there different logics that contribute to modern cacophony, but that there are variations of similar logics with different moral valences. The production of goods is different from the production of academic knowledge. Both contribute to cacophony, but one does so for remuneration, the other to contribute to the growing body of knowledge and ostensibly to "promote social progress and order." Both arguably trace their origins to the 1800s—proletarianization on the one hand, positivism on the other.

The turn of the twentieth century saw the rise of a new logic: consumerism. It doesn't replace production but is added to it. It does shift the moral valences around accumulation, however.

According to Stewart Ewen, a key event in the rise of consumerism was the invention and spread of the assembly line. This led to massive increases in the amount of products and goods that could be created. But companies discovered they could now produce more than they could sell. Ewen calls this "the social crisis of industrialization."[26] Before the problem had been how to get the masses to spend most of their lives working. Now the problem was how to get them to spend their money on consumer goods. Ewen thinks this involved a shift on the part of the wealthy and business class. Instead of seeing people as potential producers from which we should seek to extract the most amount of work for the least amount of pay, they should be seen as potential consumers of the very products they are making. Ewen quotes Mrs. Christine Fredrick:

> Consumptionism is the name given to the new doctrine; and it is admitted today to be the greatest idea that America has to give to the world; the idea that workmen and masses be looked upon not simply as workers and producer, but as consumers . . . Pay them more, sell them more, prosper more is the equation.[27]

This implies that there is a motivation for employers to no longer seek to merely pay their employees the least amount possible, but to strike a balance between increasing profits through low wages and increasing profits through selling products to the same employees that are making them, for which they need to have money. This also involves a significant shift in how workers are interpellated (what they are called and expected to be and act like), a shift in how workers think of themselves and the moral valences of accumulation. For the hard-working producer of the 1800s, it is important to scrimp and save, to be frugal and careful with spending habits. But the social crisis of industrialization means that we need these works to not save all their money, but to spend it. I recall when the 2007–8 recession occurred, then US president Bush sought to ameliorate the crisis by offering stimulus checks. But this free money needed to be spent. Bush was adamant: don't save this money, go out and buy a new TV. I remember various older family members that had been raised frugally finding this demand to go out to buy a TV in times of recession odd and misguided. They were reacting according to the older set of "scrimp-and-save" values and were alarmed at the cynical "spend-and-spend-more-to-save-(and grow)-the-economy" values.

What we see here are different moral valuations and different understandings of accumulation. In the pre-consumerism, work-hard producer mentality, one seeks to accumulate through hard work and saving (accumulating) money. But in the new consumer age, workers need to embrace new values that continues to emphasize working hard, but also emphasized playing hard (spending). Accumulation here means not only accumulating money but then using that money to accumulate consumer goods.

As the example of my frugal older relatives illustrates, this was not an easy shift for those whose morality and personal identity were tied to these older values. For Ewen and other scholars of the rise of consumerism, the obvious answer to this problem was advertising.[28]

Advertising isn't just seductive messaging designed to tempt consumers to buy stuff they don't really need. More critically, advertising seeks to create an individual who is the object of harsh and continual social scrutiny. Ewen offers various examples of the barbed, identity-directed advertisements of the early twentieth century: "Unless you are one women in a thousand, you must use powder and rouge. Modern living has robbed women of much of their color . . . taken away the conditions that once gave natural roses in the cheeks."[29] Every part of your life, every part of your body is increasingly targeted as something that may be a problem, and that can be solved through buying the right product. The self and the body now become objects that one needs to manage and fix in order to succeed in life. Failing to do so will have dire consequences:

> There will be quizzical looks, doubtful stares and critical estimates. He will be thought queer. He will be judged as lacking in brain power and, perhaps, as an undesirable person. If he persists . . . he will, if he is an employee, lose his job! He will lose customers if he is a salesman; he will lose votes if he is a politician . . . He will lose all his friends.[30]

In short, Ewen summarizes: "advertising helps to keep the masses dissatisfied with their mode of life, discontented with ugly things around them. Satisfied customers are not as profitable as discontented ones."[31]

Now we have moved far beyond this to a point where, as Zygmunt Bauman argues, we treat ourselves as a product to package and market.[32] Not only must we manage and market our physical appearance, our CVs, and our "lifestyles," but we must also do so with our digital identities.

While there is much to say about these issues, I won't belabor these points here. For our purposes in this chapter, it is enough to indicate how the logic of consumerism is added to the logic of production and the overall result is, yet again, more stuff and more cacophony.

Transgression

This brings us to the final logic I would like to address: the logic of transgression. Here we will see why looking at academia is particularly helpful in thinking through the dynamics of cacophony. To understand the logic of transgression, I will turn to Bauman again.

Bauman's work can be arguably separated into two parts: his writing on modernity and postmodernity of the 1980s and 1990s, and the shift to speaking of "solid modernity" and "liquid modernity" in the 2000s. In the later phase, he stops speaking of postmodernity.

Like other thinkers of this period, Bauman was concerned about the colonial, imperialist, and disciplinary pretentions of modernity. Inspired by Foucault and the critical theorists of the Frankfurt School, Bauman argues that the project of modernity is not as freeing as it promised, but instead stunts and constrains us to the ideals of *homo economicus*. As we saw above, Bauman articulates modernity as a kind of gardening project, which seeks to organize everything—including humans—into "proper" rows. This involves defining categories and trying to eliminate compromising ambiguities. This can be seen as functioning at many levels: with regard to gender—assigning men and women to different roles,[33] with regard to race,[34] with regard to nationality,[35] with regard to class, with regard to sexual orientation, and so on.

This was (and is), of course, very constraining and destructive for those who did not fit into or did not want to be forced into these assigned categories. This could be gay or transgender folk who did not fit into the "right" gender boxes, women who did not want to be limited to the domestic sphere, non-whites that did not want to be second-class citizens, communities that did not want to assimilate to a national culture or be forced to speak a particular language (e.g., the Basques in Spain or Mayans in Mexico), mixed-race and other individuals who fit into multiple categories (Hawaiian Americans, Turkish Germans), people only partially assimilated into the ideals of *homo economicus*, and so on.

In the 1980s, a variety of social thinkers and philosophers concerned with these issues began to talk about "postmodernity." This term is notorious for being difficult to nail down and has largely been rejected as unhelpful now, but at the time it was looked at primarily in two ways: first, as an alternative to the disciplinary project of modernity—as something better to come after it, and/or second, as a new kind of society that was already emerging. In the first case, postmodernity was ostensibly something desirable. In the second, perhaps not. Of course, these could be combined, and we could be seeing a new postmodern period emerging that was not disciplinary but problematic in other ways or one that was disciplinary in very different ways.

As you can see, this was all quite messy, and not only were there large differences among thinkers, but many "postmodern" thinkers vacillated over time about what this all meant. Because of how difficult it became to nail down what "postmodern" even meant, the term has been largely abandoned now.

We can see an example of Bauman's earlier writings. In *Postmodern Ethics*, Bauman argues that modern ethics have failed. We don't need to get into the reasons why here, but this was the assessment of many "postmodern" thinkers. What Bauman wants to answer is the concern that this leads to moral relativism and irresponsibility. He argues this is not the case at all, and, building on Levinas, argues that a postmodern ethics would be one that stops trying to put everyone in boxes and instead is open to the other in all their ambivalence:

> If postmodernity is a retreat from the blind alleys into which radically pursued ambitions of modernity have led, a postmodern ethics would be one that readmits the Other as a neighbor, as the close-to-hand-and-mind, into the hard core of the moral self, back from the wasteland of calculated interests to which it had been exiled; an ethics that restores the autonomous moral significance of proximity; an ethics that recasts the Other as the crucial character in the process through which the moral self comes into its own.[36]

The moral self is one that resists squeezing everything and everyone into established categories. Unlike modernity, which has a history of deluding itself into thinking the social and moral categories it "discovered" are universal, a postmodern ethics would respect the Other as a unique individual or thing (or event) that must be responded to in its singularity instead of through narrow, inflexible prejudices.[37]

The Other transgresses the rows of the modern garden. This can be a simple fact about the Other (they are born mixed-race) or something they are actively doing (they have chosen to change their gender identity) or a general point about any unique person not fitting perfectly into the many categorizations we make. Either way, according to Bauman, a postmodern ethics is also an act of transgression. It not only recognizes the basic fact that none of us fit modern categories exactly, but that this means that the rows of the modern garden are critically flawed and need to be transgressed.

There are multiple ways to transgress the rows of the modern garden. This could be done by liberating marginalized voices, revealing the historical origins of supposedly objective categories, inverting expected gender norms, challenging academic canons, and so on.

While the language of "postmodern" has been largely dropped, the logic of transgression has become very important in various academic disciplines and sub-disciplines. Instead of accepting modern, whitewashed histories, some scholars have sought to produce counter histories. Instead of remaining limited by traditional modern academic disciplines, some scholars have pushed for interdisciplinary approaches, innovative methodologies, and new disciplines like gender studies or African American studies. Instead of accepting canonical figures, some scholars have criticized their legacy by pointing to white supremacist positions or other problematic positions. Others have sought to open the canon up to include previously marginalized voices.

This is needed. But, as Nancy Fraser has recently pointed out, this can create problems. First, fighting the modern system leads to more cacophony, and there are immediate problems that require working together and cutting through the noise. This was the problem with which I began this book in the introduction by quoting Fraser's *Cannibal Capitalism*: "In this situation [the current global environmental crisis], safeguarding the planet requires building a counterhegemony. What is needed, in other words, is to resolve the present cacophony of opinion into an ecopolitical common sense that can orient a broadly shared project of transformation."[38]

Second, as Fraser points out in *Fortunes of Feminism*, many transgressive feminist critiques have been reappropriated, repackaged, and sold by neoliberal capitalism.[39] For example, many feminist efforts to encourage women-centered discourses and practices may have been initially met with opposition, but are now accepted and marketed heavily to. Gay rights, while still lacking in most places, are met with open arms and new products by neoliberal markets. Che Guevara shirts are for sale. The problem here is that proliferation of transgressive perspectives and practices contributes to cacophony and makes it harder to create the kind of "counterhegemony" needed to deal with, among other things, the environmental crisis.

Liquid Modernity

Fraser is not alone with this concern. It is central to Bauman's later work.

While his earlier works seemed to hope for a postmodern alternative to the disciplinary society of modernity, in his later phase he argues, like Fraser, that the transgressive efforts are now being appropriated or assimilated by a new phase of modernity. Instead of the pair "modernity—postmodernity," Bauman now offers the pair "solid modernity—liquid modernity." The old, disciplinary, gardening project modernity is now referred to as "solid modernity," and postmodernity is now referred to as "liquid modernity." Bauman argues the (now neoliberal) world has changed and that the new protean, "liquid" modernity has left behind the focus on proper gardened rows:

> The notion of an integrating community is a notion inherited from the now bygone panoptical era: it refers to the organized effort to fortify the borderline separating the "inside" from the "outside," to keep the inmates inside while barring outsiders from entry . . . . It refers to the enforcement of a uniform, monotonous, space-and time-ascribed code of conduct . . . an integrating community is essentially a conservative (conserving, stabilizing, routine-imposing, and preserving) force. It is at home in a strictly administered and tightly supervised and policed setting—which hardly describes the liquid-modern world, with its cult of speed and acceleration, novelty and change for the sake of changing.[40]

While for years intensive efforts were made by nations and corporations to turn humans into producers and later into consumers, following Foucault's lead as he analyzed biopower, Bauman argues that new strategies for managing human populations have begun to emerge:

> Whatever its pragmatic merits, the panopticon-style, "discipline, punish, and rule" way of achieving the needed/intended manipulation and routinization of behavioral probabilities [solid modernity] was, however, cumbersome, costly, and conflict-ridden. It was also inconvenient, and surely not the best choice

for the power holders, as it imposed severe and nonnegotiable constraints on the rulers' freedom of maneuver; as it transpired later, alternative and less-awkward strategies could be devised through which systemic stability . . . could be achieved and made secure.[41]

What in fact happened was the discovery, invention, or emergence of an alternative method of civilizing (a less cumbersome, less costly, and relatively less conflict-ridden method, but above all, one that gives more freedom, and so more power, to the power holders)—an alternative way of manipulating behavioral probabilities necessary to sustain the system of domination represented as social order.[42]

This new method of social control is not through Big Brother, *1984*-style force, but through Huxley's *Brave New World*, slick and entertaining style:

> The cultural managers switched from "normative regulation" to "seduction," from day-to-day surveillance and policing to PR, and from the stolid, overregulated, routine-based panoptical all-surveilling and all-monitoring model of power to domination through [the constant change of trends and possibilities]. In stark opposition to state bureaucracy, consumer markets are known to thrive on the *frailty* of routines and their rapid *supercession*—rapid enough to prevent their hardening into habit or norms.[43]

Instead of telling you who you can be and where you can go, liquid modernity will find a way to make you profitable whatever your preferences and identities. If you want to reject modern society and be a punk, there is a store for that. If you want to be a cowboy, there is a store for that. If you get tired of being a cowboy and want to learn computer programming, here is the coursework you will need to complete. Having given up on keeping everything in tight rows, liquid modernity represents a more fluid and flexible kind of social control: "Surrendering to the 'totality' is no longer a reluctantly embraced, discomforting, cumbersome, and often onerous duty but an avidly sought and eminently enjoyable entertainment."[44]

While transgression was and is often aimed at freedom, liquid modernity will accommodate these concerns and profit from these desires. Freedom and self-creation are the new name of the game (in fact, Bauman says, it is now your responsibility: everyone needs to create and market themselves). Whoever, whatever, wherever you want to be, as Adidas says, nothing is impossible:

> For the art of life, this new setting opens unprecedented vistas. Freedom of self-creation has never before achieved a similarly breathtaking scope—simultaneously exciting and frightening. Never before was the need for orientation points and guidance as strong and as painfully felt. Yet never before were firm and reliable orientation points and trustworthy guides in such short supply.... That shortage coincides with a proliferation of tempting suggestions and seductive offers of orientation and with a rising wave of guidebooks amid swelling throngs of counselors.[45]

As Bauman argues here, the new dynamics that develop in liquid modernity create a different set of problems than those in solid modernity. At first, it may appear that liquid modernity abandons the gardening pretensions of solid modernity. Ostensibly, liquid modernity embraces the logic of transgression, allows for (actually requires) freedom and self-creation, and then profits from the ensuing supernova of new products and identities. But each new identity, each new "neo-tribe" (as Bauman puts it) will tend to be only temporarily meaningful and fulfilling because, as Julian Young has argued, as long as it is articulated as an act of self-creation and individual choice, we will always know that it is *our* project that *we* have chosen and that *we* can discard and choose another.[46] In other words, as life is increasingly articulated as a DIY project, it will increasingly be experienced as untethered from anything except our own choice, which is, of course, fallible and fragile.[47] Unlike the (potentially stifling) weight of a great tradition like Christianity or Confucianism, the cacophony of life possibilities in liquid modernity is fragile and tends to be slipped into and out of with relative ease. This means that many seeking meaning and purpose in liquid modernity will tend to cycle through different life projects, often seeking futilely for something solid to stand on. Thus the "rising wave of guidebooks amid swelling throngs of counselors" in liquid modernity.

Here the dual structure of cacophony is particularly important to understand what is happening. While the new liquid-modern world of fluid identities and freedom of choice looks like a radically different world from solid modernity, it remains committed to the core of the project of modernity: the world of *homo economicus*. Rebellion and transgression of the gardening rows of solid modernity are tolerated and turned into a source of profit in liquid modernity as long as it doesn't fundamentally challenge *homo economicus*. Be whoever you want to be—as long as the economy keeps growing.

Most transgressive acts and identities are not a threat to liquid modernity and endless accumulation. There are some kinds of transgression, however, that do fundamentally challenge it. Perhaps the most obvious are commitments to defend and preserve the environment from commodification and destruction. Here we find a transgressive movement that often pushes back directly on the accumulative heart of liquid modernity, especially in branches of environmentalism that push us to stop buying, to stop consuming, to stop growing, to degrow, to slow down, to stop. Unlike many forms of transgression, stopping and slowing represent a genuine threat to liquid modernity and *homo economicus*. This is, above all, I suspect, why radical environmentalism is so frantically opposed in liquid modernity. This also explains a big part of the reason why indigenous ethics are fastidiously ignored: the demand to act with cosmic civility toward the non-human world requires a straightforward rejection of *homo economicus* and accumulation. As the phenomenon of greenwashing and the commodification of Native American imagery, products, and culture show, if environmentalism and indigenous practices and philosophies can be kept superficial and profitable, more power to them—but the moment they embrace their more radical roots and reject accumulation and exploitation of the Earth, they become an enemy and tend to be silenced.

One of the things that makes these issues particularly tricky is that the shift from solid to liquid modernity is not happening at the same rate in different places and in different people. Let me give an example. A homosexual may find that in certain communities, they are treated as a deviant who is transgressing the boundaries of the modern garden. In the United States, fear of homosexual transgression is still quite common among conservatives, especially social conservatives. More left-leaning communities will tend to be more tolerant. For moderate conservatives, especially fiscal conservatives, homosexual transgression tends to be viewed as less of a threat because what matters is accumulation. If this same individual is also a radical environmentalist, they are likely to find themselves resisted in socially conservative, moderately conservative, and even likely left-leaning communities. Accumulation must continue.

The resulting tension is that there are reactionary pushbacks against transgressive acts or transgressive individuals on the one side (solid modern) and happy capitalists awaiting the potential profitability of transgressive acts and identities on the other (liquid modernity). The needed work of fighting the former runs the risk of running straight into the latter. This is what Fraser thinks has happened with some feminists. In transgressing traditional (early twentieth-century) norms about women, some feminist pushes have gotten ensnared in the profiteering freedom of cacophonous capitalism.[48]

Not One versus Many, but One and Many versus One and Many

From the perspective of those trapped in the "proper" boxes and rows of solid modernity, transgression is a necessary and essential moral task. While significant work about those who are marginalized and silenced in modernity, the process of marginalization, the role of science and academics in the process, and so forth, has existed since the rise of the project of modernity, one peak of this resistance was the postmodern debates of the 1980s and 1990s and the post-postmodern discussions (decolonialism, subaltern studies, etc.) that remained concerned with these issues while moving beyond the language of "postmodern." Most current academics in the humanities are shaped to some degree by these issues. This means that most academics in the humanities are, to some degree, likely committed to the need for transgression.

This is to say that for the last fifty years in the humanities, there has been an ongoing, fruitful, and complicated series of discussions in the different disciplines in the humanities about transgression. Not always, but sometimes, these issues are framed in terms of a totalitarian solid modernity that is trying to gather up, forcibly enlist, and then manage human and natural resources on the one side, and the those that are defiantly resisting this process on the other side. For example, Hardt and Negri contrast "Empire" with "Multitude."[49] Simplistically, "empire" is the homogenizing modern system, and the "multitude" are the many resisting it. For Negri, the multitude, "the networked revolutionary masses and protest groups," is the force that "could bring down the empire."[50] While their analysis is sophisticated enough to recognize that "empire" has moved beyond solid modern forms of control to liquid-modern forms of control,[51] the framing of "Empire" versus "Multitude" has the unfortunate effect of making this issue look like the One versus the Many. This is a problem because consumer cacophony is not the One that needs to be resisted by the Many. It is the One (*homo economicus*) and the Many (the supernova effect), and, if Fraser is right, it cannot be defeated by more Many—there must also be a counterhegemony. In other words, the current situation is not One versus Many, but One and Many versus One and Many.

For theorists "committed to the Many" who see "the Many as a general form of emancipatory subjectivity," the idea of a counterhegemony may feel like a new One.[52] But Fraser's goal is not to silence the radical Many, but to articulate a mutual threat to all of them and the need for some degree of unity to confront cannibal capitalism. While I think Fraser is correct, I actually think she understates the problem of cacophony. If I am correct that consumer cacophony is both a One and a Many, then it no longer seems to me to make sense to resist them with only more Many. Furthermore, those radical movements that are the most radically phobic to *homo economicus*—environmentalism and indigenous movements—will need to take a more prominent role in Fraser's counterhegemony.

There is more I will need to say about this in the conclusions, but before doing so we will need to take a look at recent changes to cacophony, especially social media and the internet.

Notes

1 Hénaff, Marcel. *The Price of Truth: Gift, Money and Philosophy* (Stanford: Stanford University Press, 2010).

2 Pack, Justin. *Money and Thoughtlessness: A Genealogy and Defense of Traditions Suspicions of Money and Merchants* (New York, NY: Palgrave Macmillan, 2023).

3 Weber, Max. *The Protestant Ethic and the Spirit of Capitalism* (New York, NY: Routledge, 2002).

4 Clark, William. *Academic Charisma and the Origins of the Research University* (Chicago, IL: University of Chicago Press, 2006); Menand, Louis. *The Metaphysical Club: A Story of Ideas in America* (New York, NY: Farrar, Straus and Giroux, 2002); Bledstein, Burton J. *The Culture of Professionalism: The Middle Class and the Development of Higher Education in America* (New York: Norton, 1978); Rudolph, Frederick. *The American College and University: A History* (Athens, GA: University of Georgia, 1990).

5 Baronov, David. *Conceptual Foundations of Social Research Methods* (Boulder, CO: Paradigm Publishers, 2005), 22.

6 Descartes, Rene. "Discourse on Method." In *Modern Philosophy*, edited by Ariew, Roger and Eric Watkins (Indianapolis, IN: Hackett Publishing, 2009), 31.

7 Qtd in Stern, Fritz. *The Varieties of History from Voltaire to the Present* (New York, NY: Vintage Books, 1973).

8 Ibid.

9 Green, Anna and Kathleen Troup. *The Houses of History: A Critical Reader in Twentieth-Century History and Theory* (New York, NY: NYU Press, 1999), 4.

10 Kuhn, Thomas. *The Structure of Scientific Revolutions* (Chicago: University of Chicago Press, 1996), 36.

11 Rorty, Richard. *Philosophy and the Mirror of Nature* (Princeton: Princeton University Press, 1981).

12 Bauman, Zygmunt. *Modernity and Ambivalence* (Ithaca, NY: Cornell University Press, 1991).

13 Weber, Eugen. *Peasants Into Frenchmen: The Modernization of Rural France, 1870–1914* (Stanford, CA: Stanford University Press, 1976).

14 The spiritual commitment involved in this shift are described by Weber, Max. *The Protestant Ethic and the Spirit of Capitalism* (New York, NY: Routledge, 2002). See also Taylor, Charles. *A Secular Age* (Cambridge, MA: Harvard University Press, 2007).

15 Many feminists have analyzed this shift. See for example the discussion of "housewification" in Mies, Maria. *Patriarchy and Accumulation on a World Scale: Women in the International Division of Labour* (London, UK: Zed Books, 1999).

16 Foucault, Michel. *The History of Sexuality, Volume 1* (New York, NY: Vintage Books, 1990).

17 Scott, James C. *Seeing Like A State: How Certain Schemes to Improve the Human Condition Have Failed* (New Haven, CN: Yale University Press, 1998).

18 Bauman, Zygmunt. *Modernity and the Holocaust* (New York, NY: Cornell University Press, 2000).

19 Foucault, Michel. *Discipline and Punish* (New York, NY: Vintage Books, 1995).

20 Pack, Justin. *How the Neoliberalization of Academia Leads to Thoughtlessness: Arendt and the Modern University* (New York: Lexington Books, 2018).

21 Bauman, Zygmunt. *Modernity and Ambivalence* (Ithaca, NY: Cornell University Press, 1991).

22 Arendt, Hannah. *The Human Condition* (Chicago: University of Chicago Press, 1998).

23 Ibid., 13.

24 Ibid., 3.

25 Ibid., 13.

26 Ewen, Stewart. *Captains of Consciousness: Advertising and the Social Roots of the Consumer Culture* (New York, NY: Basic Books, 2001).

27 Ibid.

28 Strasser, Suan, *Satisfaction Guaranteed: The Making of the American Mass Market* (Washington DC: Smithsonian Books, 2004).

29 Ewen Stewart. *Captains of Consciousness: Advertising and the Social Roots of the Consumer Culture* (New York, NY: Basic Books, 2001).

30 Ibid., 95.

31 Ibid., 39.

32 Bauman, Zygmunt. *Consuming Life* (Malden, MA: Polity, 2007).

33 Pateman, Carole. *The Sexual Contract* (New York, NY: Polity Press, 1988).

34 Mills, Charles W. *The Racial Contract* (Ithaca, NY: Cornell University Press, 1997).

35 Weber, Eugen. *Peasants Into Frenchmen: The Modernization of Rural France, 1870–1914* (Stanford, CA: Stanford University Press, 1976).

36 Bauman, Zygmunt. *Postmodern Ethics* (Malden: Blackwell Publishing, 1990), 84.

37 Ibid., 215.

38 Fraser, Nancy. *Cannibal Capitalism: How Our System if Devouring Democracy, Care and the Planet—and What We Can Do about It* (New York, NY: Verso, 2022), 77.

39 Fraser, Nancy. *Fortunes of Feminism: From State-Managed Capitalism to Neoliberal Crisis* (Brooklyn, NY: Verso, 2013).

40 Bauman, Zygmunt. *Does Ethics Stand a Chance in a World of Consumers?* (Cambridge: Harvard University Press, 2008), 21.

41 Ibid., 155.

42 Ibid., 155.

43 Ibid., 203.

44 Ibid., 156.

45 Ibid., 24.

46 Young, Julian. *The Death of God and the Meaning of Life* (New York, NY: Routledge, 2003).

47 Bauman, Zygmunt. *The Art of Life* (Malden, MA: Polity Press, 2008).

48 This is the assessment of Alie Hochschild also. See Hochschild, Arlie Russel. *The Commercialization of Intimate Life: Notes from Home and Work* (Berkeley, CA: University of California Press, 2003).

49 Hardt Michael and Antonio Negri. *Empire* (Cambridge, MA: Harvard University Press, 2001).

50 Han, Byung-Chul. *Capitalism and the Death Drive* (Cambridge, UK: Polity Press, 2022), 15.

51 Deleuze, Gilles. "Postscript on the Societies of Control." *October*, vol. 59 (1992): pp. 3–7.

52 Carson, Rebecca, et al. *Politics of the Many: Contemporary Radical Thought and the Crisis of Agency* (New York, NY: Bloomsbury Publishing, 2021).

6

Social Media and Contemporary Changes

Any discussion of contemporary cacophony is going to have to deal with what is likely the primary and most deafening source of cacophony in most of our lives now: social media and the internet. There are clearly qualitative changes that result from both. For example, one of the things that makes social media different is that it doesn't just produce more content itself, so much as provide a platform on which users can provide, share, and consume their own and other's content. We buy and consume not only each other but all the weird and wonderful things we think, see, react to, despise, love to share with and about each other. This, of course leads to quantitative increases in cacophony: memes, political misinformation, music, trends, jokes, gossip, videos . . . the scale here is incomprehensible. More than perhaps anything else, social media and the internet more broadly embody cacophony and the supernova effect.

Not surprisingly, the philosophical response to social media has been fragmented and tardy. *The Stanford Encyclopedia of Philosophy* entry on "Social Media and Ethics" (first written in 2012, revision 2021) claims "the primary ethical topic areas around which philosophical reflections on SNS have, to date, converged [are]: privacy; identity and community; friendship, virtue and the good life; democracy, free speech, misinformation/disinformation and the public sphere; and cybercrime."[1] All these are important issues, but, perhaps predicably, cacophony (or "information overload," or "too much information," etc.) is missing from this list. This is not to say that recent and contemporary philosophers have not been talking about the problem of cacophony. Some have. But it does seem cacophony has been, yet again, largely lost in the cacophony.

Limiting ourselves to the problem of cacophony, the question concerning social media is not whether it is making cacophony worse. The question is whether it is crossing some threshold or causing qualitative changes that are critically significant. In other words, it is clearly more noise, more perspectives, and more possibilities, but it is more of the same? Has it passed some limit? Is there something different about cacophony now? The problem of these qualitative changes is a complex one, and it seems to me that we are only beginning to deal seriously with these issues.

For our purposes here, I have chosen to look at two thinkers who argue that we are indeed passing critical thresholds. In both cases, this causes and is caused by qualitative changes. After looking at each of these arguments, I want to turn to a concrete example of how these changes are affecting contemporary practices, in this case one with which I have had close experience: academic publishing.

The Tyranny of the Moment

The first thinker I will examine, Thomas Hylland Eriksen, is writing at the onset of social media in 2001. This might appear too early to have much to say about these issues, but I would argue that, along with Zygmunt Bauman, Eriksen's *Tyranny of the Moment: Fast and Slow Time in the Information Age* is one of the rare philosophical treatments of the problem of cacophony in the last twenty-five years. Furthermore, while thinkers writing at the onset of social changes may fail to see or foresee certain implications of the issues they are addressing, they may, on the contrary, have insights that are available to them due to the freshness of these changes. What to us is now relatively normalized to them may be new and strange. This is certainly the case with the continued influence of Heidegger, Albert Borgmann, and Hubert Dreyfus—all of whom remain key influences in the philosophy of technology and the philosophy of the internet.

For example, Heidegger, despite writing long before the internet, argued that modern technology tends to be disconnected from place (abstract), constantly accelerating, and predatory on the natural world (and on humans—Heidegger points out the significance of the phrase "human resources").[2] Together, abstraction, dislocation, acceleration, and aggressive exploitation are deadly to what he calls "meditative thinking" and instead encourage "calculative thinking." Everyone is in a money-driven hurry to get results (calculative thinking) without taking the time to think about whether we should (meditative thinking). We end up alienated from place, caught up in abstract systems, and entertained by shows about faraway places.

Heidegger's analysis has become foundational for the philosophy of technology, with contemporary thinkers tending to align with it, or do apologetic work against it. As the *Stanford Encyclopedia of Philosophy* points out, Borgmann and Dreyfus play a similar role for those writing about social media. I would suggest Bauman and Eriksen's work could play a similar role if there ever were to develop a group committed to thinking about cacophony in the age of the internet.

Eriksen summarizes his argument as follows:

> A central claim of the book is that the unhindered and massive flow of information in our time is about to fill all the gaps, leading as a consequence to a situation where everything threatens to become a hysterical series of saturated moments, without a "before" and "after," a "here" and "there" to separate them. Indeed, even the "here and now" is threatened since the next moment comes so quickly that it becomes difficult to live in the present. We live with our gaze firmly fixed on a point about two seconds into the future. The consequences of this extreme hurriedness are overwhelming; both the past and the future as mental categories are threatened by the tyranny of the moment. This is the era of computers, the Internet, communication satellites, multi-channel television, SMS messages (short text messages on GSM phones), e-mail, palmtops and e-commerce. Whenever one is on the sending side, the scarcest resource is the attention of others. When one is on the receiving side, the scarcest resource is slow, continuous time. Here lies a main tension in contemporary society.[3]

The first thing Eriksen alerts us to is the problem of cacophony. Specifically, there is now so much noise, so much calling for our attention, that he claims we become caught up in "a hysterical series of saturated moments." I find this phrasing particularly effective because it emphasizes not only that each moment is "saturated," with the implication that we often cannot fully understand what is happening, but that each saturated moment is followed quickly by another, meaning that what we were struggling to understand is gone as the next moment is upon us. This sounds like the contemporary phenomenon of doom scrolling or thumbing through reels or news articles on the phone, interested in this, intrigued by that, but rarely with enough concern, patience, or perhaps even capability of truly digesting what we are reading or seeing. When it comes to the news, many of my students report they want to understand contemporary politics but tend to be overwhelmed by the quantity of sources and misinformation and settle into a frank political illiteracy.

Erikson also claims the tyranny of the moment is a threat to "both the past and the future as mental categories." Clearly, this is the case with some social media like Snapchat, which deletes all posts after twenty-four hours. Advertising certainly leans into this, encouraging us to buy what we want and live in the moment because "YOLO" (you only live once). This also seems to fit with the general indifference to environmental issues—we tend to eat and do what we want with little thought to where or when it came from and how it will affect the future.

His claim that "the scarcest resource is the attention of others" also clearly has come true in many ways. Many forms of social media are based on our need for recognition and attention from others, creating platforms that ostensibly give us more opportunities to interact and create communities. Of course, for many, it has instead led to FOMO (fear of missing out), feeling inferior compared to others, anxiety, depression, and so on.[4] It also makes us available to advertisers who are also covetous of our attention and promise to help us get the attention of others.

There are further side-effects of these changes:

> The book is about information society and the strange social and cultural side-effects it has entailed, many of which are only obliquely related to computerisation. Economic growth and time-saving, efficiency-boosting technology may have made us wealthier and more efficient, and it may have given us more time for activities of our own choice, but there are sound reasons to suspect that it also— maybe even to a greater degree—entails the exact opposite. More flexibility makes us less flexible, and more choice makes us less free. Why do most of us have less time to spare than before, contrary to what one might expect? Why does increased access to information lead to reduced comprehension? Why are there no good, politically informed visions for the future in a society infatuated with the present and the near future?[5]

The first odd side-effect he invokes here is that while many new technologies promise us freedom, we find ourselves expected to do more and often end up with less free time and freedom than we had previously. This comes both from outside pressures and pressures we put on ourselves. The tyranny of the moment tells us we don't have enough time, and we need to get more done asap. We schedule ourselves more, try to get there faster, try to get more done . . . we buy apple watches to help us manage our time and watch our health. Throughout, Eriksen calls this a loss of "space"—which he means not only the loss of time (space) to do things, but also free space in our minds, space in our schedules, space in our attention, and so on. Everything comes to feel rushed and overwhelming.

A second side-effect is that we have more information but understand less. We don't need to belabor this point, as it is something

Ortega y Gasset also argues. Too much information becomes a *selva selvaggia* and we risk drowning in the proliferation of facts, tidbits, misinformation, and minutiae. As a result, Eriksen claims: "A crucial skill in information society consists in protecting oneself against the 99.99 per cent of the information offered that one does not want (and, naturally, exploiting the last 0.01 per cent in a merciless way)."[6] He elaborates:

> Today, the jungle has become so dense that one needs to be both stubborn and single-minded in order to be well informed about anything at all. Even someone paid by the state to do research on, say, chaos theory, cannot possibly read everything that is being written within the field, even if one restricts the scope to the English language literature. It is viable to scan titles, summaries and tables of contents into the brain, but continuous texts? Forget it.
>
> Other tasks are waiting. The next moment kills the present. The need for filters, pathfinders, organising principles for knowledge becomes overwhelming. Or does it? Is it perhaps rather the case that growing numbers of people become accustomed to living in a world where colourful fragments of information flit by, lacking direction and cohesion—and do not see this as a problem? I suspect this is happening to many of us, and if such is the case, an unintended consequence of the information revolution may be a fundamental transformation of the notion of knowledge.[7]

Ortega y Gasset argued we needed institutions like libraries and universities to take on the task of integrating and organizing knowledge so that we avoid drowning in it.[8] I have already referenced the *Stanford Encyclopedia of Philosophy* which is ostensibly doing this.

But there are, of course, technological solutions for the *selva selvaggia*, perhaps above all the search engine. At the time of writing, Artificial Intelligence has become more widespread and claims to help us sort through the jungle better than ever. But this has left quite a few disconcerting questions. What is knowledge when it is filtered and compiled by AI? How do we prevent so-called AI "hallucinations"? What if AI is just bullshitting?[9]

A third side-effect is the loss of political visions for the future. This claim harkens back to Marcuse's *One-Dimensional Man* in which he argues that the supposed superiority and freedom of consumer capitalism have left many incapable or uninterested in thinking about alternatives.[10] While this claim could still hold for many, Eriksen argues that we should add to this the exhaustion of being overwhelmed and failing to have the imagination and/or energy to challenge the *status quo*.

Part of the problem here is that the new era "creates a new existential situation for many people, who may (or have to) redefine themselves from day to day, in a context which lacks stability and predictability, where people are both free to choose and unfree not to choose."[11] We are free, but must choose; we have more information than ever, but don't know what the truth is; we are taught anything is possible, as long as we can afford it. The information society is full of these sorts of contradictions that make it "liberating and frustrating, fascinating and frightening."[12]

Taken together, Eriksen clearly thinks we have hit a critical threshold and that these changes are radically affecting the nature of knowledge, self-identity, political literacy, and so on. He emphasizes over and over the need to filter this cacophony and the need to not dump this task on each individual. While Ortega y Gasset calls on librarians and universities to take up this task, Eriksen doesn't outline a plan for exactly how this can and should be done.

How does Eriksen's argument hold up almost twenty-five years later? At a couple of points in his arguments, Eriksen discusses the growth over time of the number of books that are printed and the number of emails that are received in a year. In both cases, the number was increasing rapidly. As is the case with the 50-year-old documentary *Future Shock*, which also references the proliferation of books being published, the numbers look tiny compared to the outpouring now. But this is exactly Eriksen's point—there seems to be exponential growth with the arrival of the internet.[13]

While Eriksen is correct that many experience these changes as a "fragmentation"[14] in which "pieces replace totalities,"[15] and "coherence disappears,"[16] this is only the supernova side of consumer cacophony. The stable core of consumer cacophony—*homo economicus* and the demands of accumulation—continues to be globally foisted on all modernizing cultures. This is not to say that Eriksen is wrong, just that if we don't emphasize the homogenizing core of cacophony we may get a picture in which it seems everything falls apart without recognizing that, with regard to the core of consumer cacophony, nothing changes.

There are two takeaways from Eriksen that I think he gets correct. First, while he doesn't frame his argument against those that celebrate transgression and embrace a "politics of the many," his argument does not emphasize the liberatory power of cacophony. On the contrary, he emphasizes repeatedly the need for filtering.[17] As I argued in the last chapter, while I agree there remains a strong need for transgression in many contexts, too often this mitigates against the need for filtering. We need both transgression and filtering, and we need to be sensitive to the ways that each can harm the other.

Second, Eriksen concludes his book with a chapter on the "pleasures of slow time."[18] Doing this places him in the various slow movements. Perhaps the most well-known of these is the slow food movement,[19] but there are also advocates of slow science.[20] Eriksen agrees with these movements that the culture of speed results in the cutting of corners, simplification, and rushing—all of which often lead to bad food and bad research. Hannah Arendt puts the point this way: "Under modern conditions, not destruction but conservation spells ruin because the very durability of conserved objects is the greatest impediment to the turnover process, whose constant gain in speed is the only constancy left wherever it has taken hold."[21] In other words, the only transgression that threatens liquid modernity is conservation. The true rebel in consumer cacophony buys as little as possible.

The Crisis of Narration

Let me now turn to a second argument about social media and cacophony. While the first thinker we just examined, Eriksen, was writing at the beginning of social media twenty-five years ago, I will be using a book published the same year I am writing this by Byung-Chul Han for the second argument. *The Tyranny of the Moment* was published roughly twenty-five years after *Future Shock*. Han's *The Crisis of Narration* was published almost twenty-five years after *The Tyranny of the Moment*.

Byung-Chul Han's breakout *The Burnout Society* made him perhaps the most well-known philosopher-critic of the internet and the social media era. I will not try to offer an overview of his twenty-two books published in English since 2015 (!). For the sake of space, I will limit myself to his newest at the time I am writing this.

Like Eriksen, Han argues we have reached or are reaching a critical threshold. For Han, it is destroying narration. By "narrative," Han means more than a story. He means the kind of powerful stories that are an "anchor in being," that give us the sense of having a home, that give life "meaning, support and orientation."[22] Religion functions as such a narrative. "It *narrates* contingency away. Christian religion is a meta-narrative that reaches into every nook and cranny of life and anchors it in being. Time itself becomes freighted with narrative."[23] Here Han sounds much like Nietzsche, pointing out the ways that religious traditions give us instincts and carve out a place in the flux of reality. As Han puts it: "Narration is a *concluding form*. It creates a *closed* order that founds meaning and identity."[24]

The contrast to this he calls "storytelling." His use of the word "stories" here, refers to the digital term "stories," which are videos, pictures, or written words that appear for twenty-four hours and then disappear. Snapchat first used "Stories," and then both Instagram and Facebook copied the phrase and practice. "Stories" then are superficial, temporary narratives.

After the death of God (Nietzsche's famous phrase for, among other things, the breakdown of the influence of traditional religions in modernity), humans still needed meaning. While nationalism, cosmopolitanism, liberalism, communism, fascism, and other -isms tried to fill the God-shaped holes, Nietzsche thought modernity had ultimately failed to provide a new, powerful narrative. Han argues that capitalism has tried to do so also: "Through storytelling, capitalism appropriates the narrative and submits it to consumption."[25] Or, in perhaps the most concise statement of his argument: "In digital late modernity, we conceal the nakedness—the absence of meaning in our lives—by constantly posting, liking, and sharing. The noise of communication and information is supposed to ensure that life's terrifying vacuity remains hidden."[26] Stories provide us temporary meaning. Capitalism will gladly offer it (for a price, and only for a moment so it can profit again later).

Han also contrasts narration with information. The digital world has vastly accelerated the amount of information and stories we have access to. Clearly, Han recognizes the problem of cacophony:

Narration and information are counteracting forces. Information intensifies the experience of contingency, whereas narration reduces it by turning the accidental into a necessity... Information is additive and cumulative. It is not a bearer of sense, whereas narration carries sense. The original meaning of "sense" is direction. Today we are perfectly informed, but we lack orientation. Information also dissects time into a mere sequence of present moments

the informatization of society accelerates its de-narrativization ... amid the tsunami of information, there arises a need for meaning, identity and orientation, that is, a need *to clear the thick forest of information in which we risk losing ourselves.* The flood of ephemeral narratives, including conspiracy theories, and the tsunami of information are ultimately two sides of the same coin.

Adrift in the sea of information and data, we seek a *narrative anchor*.[27]

This quote is quite felicitous for us because Han points to both the tyranny of the moment (without invoking this phrase) and the suffocating, cacophonous thick forests (*selva selvaggia*) of information. He shows how these feed on each other. The more we seek meaning in fragmented cacophony, the more we tend to embrace and share stories, but this increases cacophony. The final claim "we seek a narrative anchor" is ambiguous and can be understood in two ways. On the one hand, it describes this desperate quest for meaning that drives story sharing and increases cacophony. On the other hand, it can amount to saying, like Fraser, that we need a counterhegemony. We need a narrative that helps us escape the cacophony of stories.

Han argues that this situation is not an accident. It is a form of domination:

[I]nformation is becoming a new form of being, even a new form of domination. Alongside neoliberalism, we are seeing the establishment of an information regime that works not through repression but through seduction. It takes on a smart form. It does not operate through imperatives and prohibitions. It does not silence us. Rather, this smart form of domination constantly asks us to communicate our opinions, needs, and preferences, to tell our lives, to post, share and like messages. Freedom is not repressed but comprehensively exploited.[28]

Here Han invokes the language of "neoliberalism" which we do not see in Eriksen. "Neoliberalism" is a word that is used by critics of the embrace of laissez-faire economic policies that began with Thatcher, Reagan, and later Clinton. The neoliberal era, which we are still in currently, is one of privatization, destruction of social safety nets, faith in markets, and deregulation. What Han claims here is that neoliberalism promises freedom and opportunity through "free" markets, while chaining us to the logic of money and markets. This goes hand in hand, he thinks, with the information societies' promise of freedom through information and communication, which we are expected to participate in and contribute to. Both neoliberalism and the information regime promise freedom and pleasure, but together elicit our labor, our consumption, our attention, our participation, and our allegiance.

His description of the "neoliberal system of rule" is strikingly similar to Bauman's description of liquid modernity. Like Bauman, he thinks we are moving away from the old solid modern rule of discipline:

> The system-preserving power [of neoliberalism] is no longer oppressive but seductive. It is no longer as clearly visible as it had been under the disciplinary regime. There is no longer a concrete opponent, no one who is taking away the freedom of the people, no oppressor to be resisted.
>
> Out of the oppressed worker, neoliberalism created the free entrepreneur, the entrepreneur of the self. Today, everyone is a self-exploiting worker in his own enterprise. Everyone is both master and slave. The class struggle has been transformed into an internal struggle against oneself. Those who fail blame themselves and feel ashamed, People see themselves, rather than society, as

the problem. Disciplinary power, attempting to control people by force, by subjecting them to a dense matric of orders and prohibitions, is inefficient. Much more efficient is that technique of power that ensures that people subordinate themselves to the system of rule voluntarily. The exceptional efficiency of this technique derives from the fact that it does not work through prohibition and deprivation but through please and fulfillment . . .

. . . Today, we expose ourselves voluntarily. It is precisely this felt freedom that makes protest impossible. Unlike those protesting against the census in the eighties [in Germany], we do not significantly resist surveillance. Voluntary self-disclosure and self-exposure follow the same principle of efficiently as voluntary self-exploitation . . .

. . . System-preserving power has now taken on a smart, friendly form, and it has thereby become invisible and unassailable. The subordinated subject is not even aware of its subordination, it believes itself to be free.[29]

Like Bauman, Han believes that the insidious power of neoliberalism comes from its ability to hyper-individualize our self and social understanding. The role of social institutions is deemphasized (despite still being used to push the neoliberal agenda), and instead responsibility is placed on each of us. This pairs well with meritocracy: each of us is responsible for our own situation. If you did not succeed, it is your fault. If you have succeeded, it was due to your efforts. Poverty is to be blamed on the poor—after all, they wouldn't be poor if they had worked harder and/or smarter. The wealth of the rich is a reflection of their virtue. They have earned their reward, there is no sense in the rest of us complaining about it. Get to work.

Han's most famous book, *The Burnout Society*, argues that these atomistic expectations lead to many expending themselves so hard that they burn themselves out.[30] In *Crisis*, Han believes this creates an atomistic situation in which we feel free, but we are isolated and adrift, unable to establish the kind of meaningful, lasting narratives we need to create flourishing communities:

> Because we lack sufficiently strong communal narratives, our late modern societies are unstable. Without a shared narrative, the *political*, which makes *shared action* possible, cannot properly form. In the neoliberal regime, the shared narrative gradually disintegrates into *private narratives, models of self-realization*. The neoliberal regime prevents the formation of community-founding narratives. In the name of performance and productivity, it separates human beings from one another. As a result, we have few narratives that could serve to found community and meaning. The proliferation of private narratives erodes community. Stories on social media, which make the private public, undermine the *political public sphere* and make the formation of shared narratives even more difficult.[31]

When Han invokes the political here, Arendt is in the background. Arendt argued, against our current normal understanding, that the political is not about managing and commanding people but working through something and making decisions together. Power is not the ability to force others to do what you want, but how compelling a particular tradition or idea is—and therefore why people choose to embrace it.³² But if a group of people does not share a coherent base set of commitments, a narrative that gives them some degree of direction and cohesion, they will not be able to work together in a shared world. Han's claim here is that neoliberalism, consumerism, and cacophony create a malignant fragmentation that is constantly breaking and adding, discarding and jumbling such that our world is a "chaotic, disorderly heap."³³

Like Nietzsche, Han thinks that we have passed into a nihilistic state that is deeply harmful: "Life in late modernity us utterly naked. It lacks narrative imagination. Pieces of information cannot be tied together into a narrative. Things thus break free. The coherence from which events derive their meaning gives way to a meaningless side-by-side and one-after-the-other. There is no narrative horizon that lifts us above mere life."³⁴

Is there a solution for Han? In this book, at least, we do not get a concrete alternative, just the affirmation that there could be a narrative that is not provincial, conservative (right-wing), and discriminatory. Han only briefly points to a Kantian-inspired, open, and hospitable cosmopolitan narrative of "perpetual peace." But he doesn't flesh this vision out, and he doesn't give us specifics about how to deal with cacophony. Eriksen tells us to slow down; Han leaves us without a way out. And this could very well be correct.

Before turning to the conclusion, I want to offer a concrete example of how the acceleration of cacophony is affecting a particular practice, in this case, academic publishing. This will, I hope, help us see the struggle to adjust to the cacophony of the age of the internet and social media (and increasingly AI).

Academic Publishing

Digital technologies often create a proliferating loop in which they enable more of something, which ends up crowding the field, which in turn leads to new strategies for gaining attention, more noise, and often more products. An easy example of this is YouTube, which allowed for the sharing of music and music videos on a scale previously unimaginable. On the one hand, this made it far easier for musicians to get their music out there and available to consumers. You can find music from around the world on YouTube, including all sorts of wonderfully obscure materials. Of course, at the same time, the exponential increase in music available means that for many musicians it becomes harder to cut through all the noise and get attention. Often the biggest musicians get more attention and fans than ever, while the majority get paid a pittance for each stream. In terms of cacophony, all this makes it ever worse.

A similar shift is happening with books, and it is radically affecting academic publishing. Books too have been digitized and can be bought and downloaded, read on Kindle, chopped into pieces, and turned into PDFs, shared, and now summarized with AI. Like music, one of the results has been an explosion of published books. What does this mean for academic books?

Different publishers have tried to deal with this in different ways. While there are scholars attempting to trace these changes in different disciplines, I want to proceed by relating my own experience with these changes both to personalize some of the difficulties involved, but also to get into some of the details in a way that a general analysis cannot.

I am not a particularly ambitious or aggressive academic, but this will be my seventh book published with six different publishers. Comparing the differences in these experiences will help illustrate the different strategies publishers are taking and how this affects (academic) authors. Since I am writing in a dying discipline in the dying humanities, the situation may be somewhat different in other disciplines, but the kinds of strategies being used here are not limited to philosophy.

I am particularly interested in how neoliberalization is affecting publishing. Recall that this term is used by critics to describe the subjection of many different aspects of modern life to the logic of money and markets. Some more prestigious publishers can afford to be less affected by neoliberalization because they are ostensibly not looking to publish books to make money, but to contribute to the growing body of knowledge. Oxford University Press, for example, is a nonprofit publisher that publishes scholarly works from authors of high renown and textbooks aimed at disseminating knowledge. Authors are not publishing here to make money (although they could be doing it to increase their esteem).

Less prestigious publishers that are seeking to profit from academic publishing are in a tighter bind. The increase in books and the digitization of books make it more difficult for them to draw attention to what they are publishing. One way of attempting to deal with this is to shift the focus of sales away from the public to libraries. This was the strategy of the first publisher I worked with, Lexington Press.

I am not a famous academic, nor am I networked with groups of famous academics. As such, I was aware that the odds of getting published by a prestigious publisher were very low. In fact, initially,

I wasn't particularly interested in trying to publish a book, but I noticed a colleague from graduate school had published a book with Lexington. Randomly curious, I called him up and asked him about his experience. He claimed to have had a good experience and encouraged me to submit something to them.

Submitting a proposal involved filling out a rather lengthy standardized form and submitting an introduction, a chapter, my CV, and so on. In my case, I was submitting my dissertation, so this was fairly easy. Since I had not been through this process before, despite my dissertation being on the neoliberalization of academia, I did not fully understand at the time how much of this procedure had been neoliberalized. For example, some publishers ask the author to provide the information of potential reviewers. This is rather odd because the author could potentially provide the names of sympathetic academic friends. But it cuts out the need for the publisher to do the work of finding out who might be a good reviewer. While this makes it easier for the publisher, it is a questionable practice in terms of finding supposedly "objective" reviewers. Doing so requires some degree of knowledge of academic subfields, which editors may or may not have, especially in cacophonous academia. Another example of neoliberalization that was obvious both from the initial proposal form and throughout the later process was the expectation that marketing would be primarily driven by the author. This too saves time and money for the publisher, and since many academic authors are desperate to get read by others and likely more aware of the particular individuals who may be interested in their work, it is a good way to attempt to reach the right audience. Lexington was very explicit and encouraging that I do this work (after all, wasn't that what

I wanted?), providing information about ways to get others to buy my book or get their libraries to buy it and instructions about marketing through social media. They encouraged me to develop a plan for marketing the book and offered a customized flyer (that included a prominent misspelling) to help with the process. Which conferences would I be attending? Which academic organizations did I belong to? Could they announce the book? Could I contact them to have them review it? What social media did I regularly use? What was my plan for marketing the book on my social media? It was very clear that this was something I needed to be doing if I cared about the book, not something they would be doing.

What I didn't fully understand at the time was that they were not looking to widely publish the book, but to sell it to libraries. This was done by making a very expensive hardback (since libraries will often pay for books that will last longer on their shelves). No cheaper paperback would be published unless a certain number of hardbacks were sold. Furthermore, I would receive no money for any sales unless a certain threshold was reached.

I had to create my own cover by picking both a template (from a provided selection) and a cover image (which had to be from a selection of stock images the publisher had purchased access to). Lexington was adamant that I not use more than 500 words in quotations from any particular work without getting permission from the publisher. If permission could not be obtained, I would be responsible for paying the necessary fees. This was not a problem in my first book, because no one bothered to edit it. When I published my second book (also with Lexington), someone did do enough editing to notice that I had quoted more than 500 words (accidentally) without permission more than once and informed me that I would need to either get permission or pay the fees. I contacted one publisher who gave permission (I had to provide email proof to Lexington), but another would not and was extremely aggressive about getting the email information of my publisher. They assured me that it would be no hassle for me and that they would work the issue out between publishers. Having already been through the publishing process once, I was more sensitive to the ways everyone was seemingly trying to make money in the process, and I called this publisher out for seeking to squeeze every penny out of permissions. They repeated through a series of emails that I didn't need to worry about it and that I just needed to give them the name of my publisher and editor, and they would resolve it. I got quite annoyed and scolded them again for being greedy and discouraging me from using their author. It was just standard practice: give us the name of your publisher and contact info for your editor, they repeated. I didn't respond but was amused to see they sent multiple follow up email seeing this information, even though I was no longer responding. I cut the quotes down to less than 500 words.

Academic publishers send proposals and final edits of books out for reviews. This is supposed to ensure the quality of work. With my first book, I never heard or saw any feedback from reviewers in either case. With my second book, they did mention suggestions and grammatical corrections from a reviewer who had gone through the final edit, but they didn't bother to send me the file with grammatical corrections until I asked for it.

For both of these books, the editors had strong views about the titles. The first book was originally entitled *Academics No Longer Think*—the title of my dissertation and one I still love—but they wanted me to change it since this may be perceived as insulting to the very audience who was most likely to read it (and thus reduce sales). I ended up changing the title of the first book to the much less interesting *How the Neoliberalization of Academia Leads to Thoughtlessness*. They didn't like the title of the second book, *Amor Mundi*, because it is in Latin, and no one would understand it or know what the book was about (and therefore not buy it). Since it was an important reference to Hannah Arendt, I fought hard to keep the title, and after a long battle, they resigned themselves to few sales.

Both my first and second books sold very few copies, neither sold enough to merit a paperback publication, and I have never seen a penny for either.

My third book was a very different experience. It came about quite randomly when a publisher representative stopped by my office seeking to get me to use books for my courses from their press (this used to happen before the Covid pandemic, now it is just done via email). The publisher representative had found out what courses I was teaching and was trying to show me textbooks their press offered for those courses to get me to adopt them. Textbooks are very different from academic monographs. If a publisher can get a professor to adopt them for a course, this can result in multiple sales potentially over multiple semesters since every student will be required to purchase a copy.

The representative asked if I was using a textbook for my environmental ethics course. I was not, because I did not like the ones that were available. She said she understood and mentioned that many other professors teaching the same course had told them the same thing and that their editor was looking to create a new and different textbook. I expressed interest, and she left me his email.

Everything about this book was more thorough and more professional. This was because the strategy of selling textbooks is different from the strategy of selling monographs to libraries. The review of the initial proposal was far more thorough, getting feedback from the editor and four reviewers. There was good feedback throughout the writing of the text, and the final edit was also read by a sensitivity reader and four more reviewers. The cover was custom designed in-house (and very well done), and additional images were used inside the book to make it more attractive. The publisher took care of most of the marketing.

Why was this experience so different? Since Broadview was looking to get this book adapted as widely as possible in courses, it needed to look good and be attractive. Instead of only releasing a hardback that was prohibitively expensive, they released an affordable paperback. People could actually buy the book if they wanted to! I receive royalties for each copy sold.

While I was treated far more ethically by this publisher, it should be pointed out that they also had a strategy for dealing with the cacophony of books. Instead of trying to make money from libraries, they sought to make money by getting the book adopted in courses. This necessitates producing a higher quality product that will be attractive to teachers and students alike. Both the library strategy and the textbook strategy have their risks. The library strategy is low risk, low reward. If libraries don't buy enough copies, there will not be much profit. It makes sense to not bother investing much in the book and push most of the work off onto the author. The textbook strategy is higher risk, higher reward. If enough professors adopt the text, there could be many sales. Therefore, the publisher must invest more time and money into making sure the book is high quality and attractive.

During the pandemic, I wrote a fourth book. This was a labor of love, and I wanted more than anything else to have it be available in an affordable paperback. Palgrave Macmillan was the first publisher to show interest in it. The review process ended up being quite lengthy, as the initial reviewer had many comments and suggestions. They thought the book had potential but needed to reference a large body of literature that was missing. The editor suggested I review this literature and resubmit the proposal. After a year, I did so. While incorporating these suggestions, I had continued to write the book since I had lots of time during the pandemic. Eventually, they offered me a contract; although, to my chagrin, it turned out they had adopted the library model and would only publish a very expensive hardback and a very expensive paperback. The paperback was guaranteed to be published after one year (not contingent upon sales), but it would not be affordable. Disappointed, I turned down the offer.

I continued working on the book and shopping it around for another year, but didn't get any interest. After a year, a different editor from Palgrave Macmillan contacted me. The previous editor had moved to a different position, and the new editor was interested to know why I hadn't accepted their offer. I mentioned that it was important for me to have an affordable paperback so people could actually buy the book instead of just libraries. She argued that while both the hardback and paperback would be prohibitively expensive, the book would also be included in a package of books that they were selling to libraries, and that digital copies of the book would be widely available through libraries. This was a new strategy I had not seen before. They wanted my book, not to sell by itself to libraries, but because they wanted it as part of a batch of books, and they were selling access to all these books as part of a package deal. A library may or may not be interested in my book, but they may be interested in the overall package. If my book helped make the overall package more attractive, it was worth it for the publisher. I recognized this was just as exploitative as the Lexington approach, but I loved this book, and I was tired of shopping it around. I ended up accepting the contract because I would rather see the book published than not at all. As I expected, they gave the book slightly more attention than Lexington did. I was not treated much better. I received a one-time payment of $800 and will receive no royalties. It turns out whatever package deal they are offering has not been bought by many libraries. It is basically impossible for potential readers to get an affordable copy of this book.

I published a fifth book, and it is also revealing about the strategy of book publishers. This book was written for a progressive religious press that is fairly academic. Their strategy is to use Amazon to publish cheap paperback copies. Amazon has started a revolutionary self-publishing business. Authors create digital copies of their work, create a cover, and then upload this to Amazon. Amazon can then print it on demand or provide digital copies. They charge a certain rate for printed materials and less for digital copies. For an academic author, this had two advantages. First, they can avoid the cumbersome process of peer review. Obviously, this is going to make many academics nervous because the peer review process is meant to assure the quality of academic work. With no checks, an academic could publish all sorts of nonsense. There is a second advantage for academic authors: royalties for self-published works on Amazon can be far higher than with a traditional press. For nonacademic authors, this process can help to avoid dealing with agents who often act as gatekeepers. Many authors can't find receptive agents, so self-publishing allows them to publish something they might never have been able to otherwise. It should be mentioned that there is a whole industry of helping self-published authors market their books and advertise on social media. Facebook, Instagram, and TikTok provide relatively easy means of advertising—for a fee, of course. Essentially, one pays to have themselves inserted into the algorithm these sites are using for a period of time.

I did not realize this press was using Amazon to publish their books initially. I would describe my experience as an author as better than Lexington and Palgrave Macmillan, but not as good as Broadview. My proposal went through a typical review, and the short, finished book was also sent out for review and then given two rounds of editing. The cover was custom designed and attractive.

By using Amazon self-publishing, this publisher can drastically cut down on costs. They only have to pay their editors and cover artist(s). In fact, they are a nonprofit, and whatever money is left after Amazon takes its cut goes to the author. This approach was quite different from the other publishers I have worked with because it is clearly not designed to drive profits. Nonetheless, it was clear that a hybrid publisher could take advantage of Amazon and other platforms for self-publishing to cut costs while preserving academic integrity through the peer review process.

What to make of all this? Clearly, for-profit academic publishers are struggling to remain profitable as the amount of books and digital writing increases. When there is so much more to watch, click, and read, people simply read less. When people become accustomed to reading snippets and tweets, longer works tend to be ignored—tldr—or summarized by AI.

The two authors we have looked at in this chapter, Thomas Hylland Eriksen and Byung-Chul Han, both argue that we have reached a critical threshold with cacophony. Eriksen argues we need to begin to pay attention to the philosophical problem of cacophony, take seriously the problem of filtering so much information, and slow down. Han argues... we are in trouble. I have tried to offer a concrete example of how academic publishing is trying to deal with, and of course contributing to, cacophony. These attempts are comically desperate and unfortunately reflect the woeful thoughtlessness of our situation.[35] The self-publishing of books has led to yet another incredible jump in the among of book published annually—and I haven't even touched the effects of Artificial Intelligence, which have flooded book agents with AI-produced texts. We simply are not thinking about our situation.

In the conclusions that follow, let me make an attempt to suggest some of the changes we need to consider.

Notes

1 https://plato.stanford.edu/entries/ethics-social-networking/. Accessed August 4, 2024.

2 Heidegger, Martin. "Memorial Address." *Discourse on Thinking* (New York, NY: Harper & Row, 1966).

3   Eriksen, Thomas Hylland. *Tyranny of the Moment: Fast and Slow Time in the Information Age* (Las Vegas, NV: Pluto Press, 2001), 2–3.

4   https://www.gse.harvard.edu/ideas/usable-knowledge/17/12/social-media-and-teen-anxiety. Accessed August 4, 2024.

5   Eriksen, Thomas Hylland. *Tyranny of the Moment: Fast and Slow Time in the Information Age* (Las Vegas, NV: Pluto Press, 2001), 4.

6   Ibid., 17.

7   Ibid., 20.

8   See Ch 2.

9   https://www.scientificamerican.com/article/chatgpt-isnt-hallucinating-its-bullshitting. Accessed August 20, 2024.

10 Marcuse, Herbert. *One Dimensional Man: Studies in the Ideology of Advanced Industrial Society* (Boston, MA: Beacon Press, 1991).

11 Eriksen, Thomas Hylland. *Tyranny of the Moment: Fast and Slow Time in the Information Age* (Las Vegas, NV: Pluto Press, 2001), 28.

12 Ibid., 28.

13 Ibid., 84.

14 Ibid., 106.

15 Ibid., 108.

16 Ibid., 137.

17 Ibid., 105.

18 Ibid., 147.

19 https://www.slowfood.com/. Accessed September 1, 2024.

20 Berg, Maggie and Barabara K. Seeber. *The Slow Professor: Challenging the Culture of Speed in the Academy* (Toronto, CA: The University of Toronto Press, 2016).

21 Arendt, Hannah. *The Human Condition* (Chicago: University of Chicago Press, 1998), 253.

22 Han, Byung-Chul. *The Crisis of Narration* (Cambridge, UK: Polity Press, 2024), vii.

23 Ibid., viii.

24 Ibid., ix.

25 Ibid., ix.

26 Ibid., 30.

27 Ibid., x.

28 Ibid., 7.

29 Han, Byung-Chul. *Capitalism and the Death Drive* (Cambridge, UK: Polity Press, 2022), 16–17.

30 Han, Byung-Chul. *The Burnout Society* (Cambridge, UK: Polity Press, 2010).

31 Han, Byung-Chul. *The Crisis of Narration* (Cambridge, UK: Polity Press, 2024), 64.

32 Arendt, Hannah. *The Human Condition* (Chicago: University of Chicago Press, 1998).

33 Han, Byung-Chul. *The Crisis of Narration* (Cambridge, UK: Polity Press, 2024), 40.

34 Ibid., 30.

35 Pack, Justin. *How the Neoliberalization of Academia Leads to Thoughtlessness: Arendt and the Modern University* (New York: Lexington Books, 2018).

Conclusion

In August of 2020, the American Food and Drug Administration released a warning on their social media that said: "You are not a horse. You are not a cow." This was in response to the bizarre phenomenon of people rushing to obtain horse dewormer to try and prevent or stop Covid-19.[1] Millions of people were dying from Covid and somewhere in the cacophony of the internet, someone got the idea that putting ivermectin in your armpits was a possible answer.

Remember that this occurred in the last year of the first term of the presidency of Donald Trump, who for four years had been unleashing a daily torrent of bullshit. It is tempting to put "lies and misinformation" instead of "bullshit" in the last sentence, but I use bullshit here as a technical term. The philosopher Harry Frankfurt has argued that "bullshitting" is not lying, but making claims without regard for truth or falsity—just asserting whatever one wants.[2] Many political commentators, and Frankfurt himself, argued that Trump is a serial bullshitter.[3] For Frankfurt, bullshitting is uniquely dangerous because it undermines the commitment to truth. If there is no truth and no falsity, we can assert anything we want, and nothing really means anything. This would be, he thinks, nothing short of the undermining of civilization.

One of the odd and alarming results of Trump's bullshitting was that it protected him. There was such a cacophony of constant bullshit coming from Trump and others that he could say the stupidest, racist, sexist, most absurd things only to have it be buried in the next day's flood of nonsense. Statements and scandals that would have crushed any other politician didn't stick, because they were washed away in the next deluge. Trump's defenders would deny he said things that everyone heard him say the week before. Stupid gaffes were excused as "alternative facts." Criticism was "Trump derangement syndrome." It was exhausting.

When Covid broke out in the last year of his presidency, he was clearly concerned, above all, with how it would affect his chances of reelection. He insisted Covid would just go away. He fought against the advice of the head of the NIAID (National Institute of Allergy and Infectious Diseases), Dr. Fauci, and cast doubt on medical science. Eventually, this led to an absurd battle about masks in public and public schools, with Trump-supporting conservative governors rejecting mask mandates and seeking to reopen schools and public areas sooner than was medically advisable.

It was in this politicized cacophony of bullshit that horse dewormer emerged as a potential savior. Despite the exasperated warnings of medical scientists, it disappeared off the shelves. (One of my students who was working on a ranch at the time later reported that they couldn't find dewormer for their horses.) Watching this unfold was simultaneously unbelievable and entirely predictable. Which conservative relative would die next because they refused to get vaccinated or because they turned to medicine for horses?

This whole situation reminded me of a passage from Kierkegaard:

It happened that a fire broke out backstage in a theatre. The clown came out to inform the public. They thought it was a jest and applauded. He repeated his warning, they shouted even louder. So I think the world will come to an end amid general applause from all the wits, who believe it's a joke.[4]

In Kierkegaard's early books, he uses pseudonyms to explore different forms of living. In *Either/Or*, which this passage comes from, he writes as "A," who is an aesthete. "A" lives life seeking pleasure and enjoyment. He is a smart and witty individual, but also somewhat lost. Not always sure what is true, he can laugh at the absurdity of the clown on stage but also appreciate the irony of doing so because he is not sure any of us knows the truth. In this little story about the clown warning everyone that the theater is burning down, is "A" the clown? Is "A" in the audience, watching their misguided reaction to the clown? Or is he outside of the events, watching the tragedy? Is he laughing with or at them? It is not clear.

For Kierkegaard, the life of an aesthete makes sense at one level. When life is as absurd as it seems, why not try to enjoy it? Like a butterfly, "A" moves here to there, trying this, trying that. On the other hand, Kierkegaard believes the aesthete ultimately fails because they cannot find anything solid, and they will end up in despair.

Almost 200 years later, Kierkegaard's aesthete reads like a person making the best of being lost in cacophony. Not sure if there is such a thing as big "T" truth, "A" will make the most of modern life, enjoying what he can and laughing at the absurdity of it all.

The fellow applying horse dewormer to his armpits to prevent Covid is also lost in cacophony. He is not sure exactly what the truth is. He knows that you can't trust the "lamestream" media because it has "Trump Derangement Syndrome." He knows that Dr. Fauci isn't a real doctor. He is torn about Covid. On the one hand, he has heard it isn't that big a deal, and he is angry that people are trying to take away his freedom with mask mandates. But he also knows people that have been hospitalized from Covid and others that have died. The liberal media might mock it, but who is to say ivermectin might not work? Better to be open-minded than to just do what you are told.

Now imagine the world's top scientists coming out and declaring a climate emergency. Will they be laughed at like "A"'s clown? Will they be dismissed as "fake news"? Will we do something about it after we stream the next season of the Lincoln Lawyer? Will we add this to the list of concerns, after the economy and "illegal" immigration? Will we even hear the scientists in the cacophony?

Of course, this is exactly what is happening. Climate scientists are demanding we act now, and not much is happening. While there are many issues contributing to this failure, I think that cacophony is a major part of the problem. Despite this, there seems to me to be very little discussion of cacophony.

Not everyone will agree that cacophony is a problem. For capitalists, it is a dream come true. For liberals, it could be seen as offering more freedom and opportunity. For some advocates of transgression or the many, it could be seen as a counter to the totalitarian pretensions of (solid) modernity.

As such, in the first three chapters, I tried to show the critical danger of cacophony by looking at three philosophers: Nietzsche, Ortega y Gasset, and Arendt. In doing this, I am interested both in the specific arguments made by each of these authors about cacophony but also trying to show that cacophony has indeed been considered a critical problem historically. This, in turn leads to the question of why, if cacophony has been a recognized problem historically, it seems to not be so now. I dealt with the criticisms of cacophony from these three thinkers in the first three chapters and then turned to the question of why cacophony doesn't seem to be taken seriously in chapters four and five. Let me briefly remind you of these arguments.

Of the thinkers of cacophony, Nietzsche is particularly interesting because he offers an initial outline of what I have been calling the "dual structure of consumer cacophony" when he argues that modern nihilism is a product both of the breakdown of instincts on the one hand and the entrenchment of bad instincts on the other hand. Nietzsche believes humans are animals, and we are far less rational than many modern figures want to think—instead, much of what we do is driven by instincts. Instincts are, to a large degree, shared by communities and traditions. But the destruction and breakdown of traditions in modernity have led to the fragmentation and chaos of instincts. Worse, the instincts that modernity has sought to instill in us are life denying and bad. The result is a dual nihilism that is simultaneously a chaos of instincts swirling around a core of vacuous, calculative, money-driven instincts.

Perhaps more than any other philosopher, Ortega y Gasset is deeply concerned about cacophony, especially as Spain sought to modernize and was threatened by a flood of information, media, and practices from other countries. O&G (Ortega y Gasset) argues that the death of cultures is often the result of choking in the *selva selvaggia*. As a result, O&G is particularly worried about the need to filter and manage information. The goal for O&G is not manipulative censorship, but the necessary management of cacophony. He calls for universities and libraries to make this problem central to their missions.

For Arendt, cacophony is a threat to worlds. She was one of the first philosophers to see the danger of modern consumerism. To use her terminology, modernity inverts traditional orders and embraces the consumeristic logic of *animal laborans*. As the logic of *homo faber* fades, we increasingly build nothing to last and be stable. Worlds themselves become the object of consumption, and humans are left without stable worlds to maintain meaning and identity. Most of us are carried along in the "onslaught of the new."

Why, if major philosophers were voicing concerns about cacophony, is there so little discussion of it now? In Chapters 4 and 5, I offered two reasons: (1) at a general level, the dual structure of cacophony and (2) at an academic level, the logic of transgression. The dual structure of cacophony refers to (A) the supernova effect and (B.1) the stable core of the world of *homo economicus* or, to use another metaphor, (B.2) the stable logics that suffuse and drive forward the supernova effect (these are two ways of describing the same thing or two parts of the same thing). While the supernova effect can be disorienting and destructive, the stable core/logics function like the invisible hand—assuring us that there are reasons for what is happening, and, especially in the form of meritocracy, that everything should be this way. The claim that "everything is falling apart" can be countered with the assuring "there is a reason for everything."

In Chapter 5, I examined four "logics" that drive cacophony: production, accumulation, consumption, and transgression. While the first three are relatively explanatory, the last part of chapter five sought to clarify what I mean by "transgression." I argued that for the last fifty years there has been an intense concern in academia, especially (or at least) in the humanities, with the totalitarian pretension of the project of modernity. Bauman describes this as the gardening project of (solid) modernity, which seeks to remake humanity in the image of *homo economicus* and place all people and things into their proper rows. Not only has this contributed to the destruction of indigenous cultures, but it has involved racism, sexism, classism, antipathy to LGBTQ people, disregard for the environment, etc. Against this, there has arisen a logic of transgression that seeks to expose these prejudices and free the oppressed.

Transgression is clearly deeply needed and continues to be needed today, but, as Bauman and Fraser argue, consumer capitalism is no longer threatened by most transgression but embraces and capitalizes it. For Bauman, transgression is no longer a threat but an engine of profit in liquid modernity. This doesn't mean that transgression is no longer necessary, but that it is fraught. Many academics in humanities see transgression as a fundamental task and the resulting cacophony as a moral good over and against the totalizing pretensions of (solid) modernity. Fraser's plea for counterhegemony argues that this is no longer true in the context of cannibal capitalism. Pushing boundaries all-too-often feeds the monster.

I indicated above that the three groups that might not agree that cacophony is a problem are capitalists, liberals, and advocates of transgression or the Many. If the arguments I have presented in this book are not fully convincing, I think there is one that stands above the others in terms of it being foundational: the environmental crisis.

This critical problem needs to be placed first and foremost, not only because it concerns the very condition for the possibility of our existence—the Earth—but also because it directly challenges the anthropocentrism of capitalism and liberalism (although it should be mentioned that capitalism is not anthropocentric but capital-centric). When capitalists claim capitalism is good, they mean it is supposedly good for humans. When liberals extoll freedom, they mean the freedom of humans. Often accumulation and human freedom come at the expense of the environment. This is due to direct exploitation of the Earth for resources, but also the failure to include non-human persons and places in the moral imaginary of anthropocentric capitalists and liberals. To be clear, capitalism and liberalism are causes (but not the sole causes) of the contemporary environmental crisis since they allow for the destruction of the Earth for accumulation and human freedom. Their anthropocentrism makes it difficult for us to see and care about non-human persons and places.

But what about advocates of transgression or the Many?

Back in 1982, Murray Bookchin complained with regard to the environmental crisis: "We can no longer afford to remain captives to the tendency of the more traditional sciences to dissect phenomena and examine their fragments. We must combine them, relate them, and see them in their totality as well as their specificity."[5] Julian Young calls the move toward breaking apart and fragmentation "centrifugal" and the move of combining and relating "centripetal."[6] Using these terms, Bookchin is saying environmentalists are spending too much time doing centrifugal work and not adequately doing centripetal work.

This is similar to the Nancy Fraser quote at the opening of this book. In *Cannibal Capitalism,* Fraser claims: "In this situation [the current global environmental crisis], safeguarding the planet requires building a counterhegemony. What is needed, in other words, is to resolve the present cacophony of opinion into an ecopolitical common sense that can orient a broadly shared project of transformation."[7] While Bookchin is addressing environmentalists, Fraser is addressing members of radical movements including feminists, environmentalists, antiracists, critical theorists, and supporters of democracy, who are doing critically important centrifugal work, but, she seems to be arguing, have failed to adequately come together and create the needed counterhegemony.

In Chapter 5, I argued that transgression is often narrated as opposition to the One, such that transgressive acts and transgressive philosophies are seen as a Many fighting against the One. I argued that this is a bad understanding of consumer cacophony because it is not just a One, but a One and a Many. The One is the (B.1) the stable core of the world of *homo economicus* and the (B.2) the stable logics that suffuse and drive forward the supernova effect. The Many is the cacophonous supernova. I see Bookchin and Fraser arguing that we can't just oppose the One of cannibal capitalism with centrifugal transgression, but we also need to oppose the Many of cannibal capitalism with centripetal integration to form a counterhegemony.

We don't need to think of centripetal integration as monolithic either. Fraser seeks to relate and combine—without dissolving—various radical movements with a counter image and a counterhegemony to cannibal capitalism:

> Whereas capitalist societies subordinate the imperatives of social, political, and ecological reproduction to those of commodity production, itself geared to accumulation, socialists need to

turn things right side up—to install the nurturing of the people, the safeguarding of nature, and democratic self-rule as societies' highest priorities, which trump efficiency and growth, In effect, socialism must put squarely in the foreground those matters that capital relegates to is disavowed background.[8]

Regardless of whether this is an adequate counterhegemony, my claim is that Fraser is right to point to the need for centripetal work.

There are, of course, different kinds of centripetal work. Let me briefly examine two. One involves the compilation, organization, streamlining and presentation of information. At first blush, this is what Ortega y Gasset seems to argue needs to be the mission of the university and the librarian. Han Byung-Chul calls for something different, what we could call narrative work. Recall that for Han, narratives give life "meaning, support and orientation."[9] Like Nietzsche, he argues humans need ways to simplify the world to make it comprehensible and meaningful. Arendt argues that this kind of coherent simplification is precisely what a (human) world is—thus we can speak of the world of "Rome," or "Athens," or the "Apache."

It would be a mistake to think of narrative work as either romantic or unnecessary. Nor will any particular world be without tensions. In fact, in cacophonous modernity we are born into multiple worlds that overlap and form a web of tensions that pull us in different directions. For example, Robin Wall Kimmerer discusses the tensions between her Native American world and her work as a scientist.[10] Gloria Anzaldua famously pointed to the tensions as a lesbian Mexican American caught in a liminal space between Mexican and American cultures.[11] There are tensions both inside worlds and tensions between worlds—how we understand this depends on how we describe and understand the boundaries of worlds. We could describe tensions between Jesuits and Dominicans as tensions between two different worlds or as tensions within the world of Christianity. And these tensions can manifest as aesthetic, moral, epistemic, metaphysical, and so forth.

Centripetal narrative work—work that puts pieces together with attention to their moral and existential significance—can be done in different ways. How it can or should be done depends on, among other things, how much faith we have in the human ability to make these things transparent to ourselves. For Nietzsche, we can only do so to a certain degree—intellectually examining instincts will tend to kill them after all. On this reading of Nietzsche, the "revaluation of values" he seeks will not be done by thinking more about values, but by a new world historical figure like Jesus, the Buddha, or Confucius founding new values—that is, a new world. If we understand Nietzsche this way, then the search for the *übermensch* can be understood as the search for someone who could found a new, hopefully life-affirming world. But such a world historical founder cannot be summoned because merely we need them. It might seem that smashing all the idols will create a vacuum that can help precipitate a new world, but there are no guarantees. Perhaps it will just create a deeper nihilism.

Even if Nietzsche is correct, this doesn't mean that scholars can't make an effort to articulate the tensions in or between worlds in a narrative form. Charles Taylor has done this in *Sources of the Self* and *A Secular Age*.[12] Both of these texts are grand narratives that seek to explore the tensions between different threads of modern identity. In fact, *Sources of the Self* even distinguishes between more instinctual "hypergoods" and surface level goods.[13] The kind of narrative work done by Taylor is both committed to the One and the Many. It does centripetal narrative work without totalitarian pretensions. He wants to promote the right kind of transgression without rejecting narrative work as totalitarian.

Both forms of centripetal work—(1). the compilation, organization, streamlining and presentation of information and (2). narrative work—are deeply needed in our current cacophony. Scholars do engage in some different forms of centripetal information work. The summary of the "current literature" that occurs at the beginning of most papers does centripetal work in order to clarify the salience of a particular academic question or problem. Some scholars work on entire books that attempt to summarize a particular sub-discipline or a particular theoretical approach. This can take the form of an introductory text for students or a compilation of the current state of a particular discourse for scholars. Undergraduate and graduate courses often function in a similar way, introducing students to key papers, works, and authors of a particular sub-field.

This centrifugal work is often preambulatory to the "real" work; however, the production of new information. This reflects the overwhelmingly positivist structure of academia—a structure that persists despite the ill standing of positivism. I have written at length elsewhere about how the ghosts of positivism continue to deeply inform academic work in a way that reflects a pervasive and worrying thoughtlessness in academia.[14] A large part of the reason for the failure to change these antiquated practices is the culture of productivity that dominates not only academia but modern society in general. Positivism and the culture of productivity combine so insidiously in modern academia that even though one pillar of this monster has collapsed, the structure remains standing and has been reinforced with the rise of neoliberalism.

This raises the question of the need for an ethics of academic production. Too many academics keep producing ever more information not only because the lingering ghost of positivism treats it as a morally good and important thing to do, but perhaps more fundamentally or more practically because the toxic neoliberal culture of productivity demands they show they are contributing something useful and, especially, profitable.

Stupidly, we keep expecting academics to publish (new and profitable work) or perish despite the critical need for centripetal work with information and narratives and without much regard for the differences of disciplines. Perhaps in a discipline in which research is cumulative, we can justify this never-ending production, but in the humanities and social sciences, academic production does not simply mirror reality but often proliferates it. In the context of cacophony, it is questionable whether academic production of this kind is ethical. Perhaps it is morally wrong to publish.[15]

The parallel with the environmental crisis is striking. We need to produce less and produce smarter. The degrowth and slow movements have both made these sorts of claims. Berg and Seeber have even applied this to academia in *The Slow Professor*.[16] A key part of producing smarter needs to be a critical emphasis on (1). the compilation, organization, streamlining and presentation of information and (2). narrative work. This requires a different set of skills than typical academic work (reading widely instead of mostly narrowly, writing about big problems instead of small ones, integrating instead of adding more). These skills and practices are institutionally discouraged in favor of "productive" and "profitable" work. There is no reason to believe the neoliberal university would ever genuinely encourage integration and narrative work precisely because it is slow, complex, and not profitable. And this is only speaking of academia. The culture of production is so entrenched in modern practices; it is hard to imagine consumer capitalist societies making any effort to take questions of meaning and fulfillment in our nihilistic and atomistic society seriously. A government agency devoted to the question of what makes life more meaningful? We just leave it up to everyone to try and figure it out for themselves and call that freedom.

It is a surreal and absurd experience to write a book about cacophony that is all but guaranteed to be swept away in the cacophony. I suspect any hope to push the juggernaut in a better direction is delusional. Nonetheless, I hope that this book has encouraged the reader to "think what we are doing," as Arendt put it.[17] I hope it encourages us to engage in the kind of centripetal work that the thinkers I have examined in this book have correctly, I think, encouraged us to engage in.

Notes

1 https://www.uclahealth.org/news/article/what-is-ivermectin-how-a-livestock-de-wormer-became-a-rumored-covid-19-aid-with-bad-side-effects. Accessed October 18, 2024.

2 Frankfurt, Harry G. *On Bullshit* (Princeton, NJ: Princeton University Press, 2005).

3 https://time.com/4321036/donald-trump-bs/; https://www.vox.com/policy-and-politics/2017/5/30/15631710/trump-bullshit. Accessed October 18, 2024.

4   Kierkegaard, Soren. *Either/Or, Vol. 1* (Princeton, NJ: Princeton University Press, 1971), 30.

5   Bookchin, Murray. *The Ecology of Freedom: The Emergence and Dissolution of Hierarchy* (Oakland, CA: AK Press, 2005), 85.

6   Young, Julian, ed. *Individual and Community in Nietzsche's Philosophy* (New York, NY: Cambridge University Press, 2014).

7   Fraser, Nancy. *Cannibal Capitalism: How Our System if Devouring Democracy, Care and the Planet—and What We Can Do about It* (New York, NY: Verso, 2022), 77.

8   Ibid., 152.

9   Han, Byung-Chul. *The Crisis of Narration* (Cambridge, UK: Polity Press, 2024), vii.

10 Kimmerer, Robin Wall. *Gathering Moss: A Natural and Cultural History of Mosses* (Corvallis, OR: Oregon State University Press, 2003).

11 Anzaldúa, Gloria. *Borderlands/La Frontera: The New Mestiza* (San Francisco, CA: Aunt Lute Books, 2012).

12 Taylor, Charles. *Sources of the Self: The Making of Modern Identity* (Boston, MA: Harvard University Press, 1992); Taylor, Charles. *A Secular Age* (Cambridge, MA: Harvard University Press, 2007).

13 Taylor, Charles. *Sources of the Self: The Making of Modern Identity* (Boston, MA: Harvard University Press, 1992).

14 Pack, Justin. *How the Neoliberalization of Academia Leads to Thoughtlessness: Arendt and the Modern University* (New York: Lexington Books, 2018).

15 Pack, Justin. "Is It Morally Wrong to Publish?" in *Philosophical Interventions in Neoliberal Higher Education* (Lexington Press, forthcoming, 2025).

16 Berg, Maggie and Barabara K. Seeber. *The Slow Professor: Challenging the Culture of Speed in the Academy* (Toronto, CA: The University of Toronto Press, 2016).

17 Arendt, Hannah. *The Human Condition* (Chicago: University of Chicago Press, 1998), 5.

BIBLIOGRAPHY

Annett, Anthony M. *Cathonomics: How Catholic Tradition Can Create a More Just Economy*. (Washington DC: Georgetown University Press, 2022).
Arendt, Hannah. *Between Past and Future*. (New York: Penguin Classics, 2006).
Arendt, Hannah "Culture and Politics." *Reflections on Literature and Culture*. (Stanford, CA: Stanford University Press, 2007).
Arendt, Hannah. *Eichmann in Jerusalem*. (New York: Penguin Classics, 2006).
Arendt, Hannah. "Philosophy and Politics." *Social Research*, Vol. 57, No. 1 (Spring 1990).
Arendt, Hannah. *The Human Condition*. (Chicago: University of Chicago Press, 1998), 295.
Arendt, Hannah. *The Life of the Mind*. (New York, NY: Harcourt Brace Jovanovich, 1978).
Baronov, David. *Conceptual Foundations of Social Research Methods* (Boulder, CO: Paradigm Publishers, 2005).
Basso, Keith H. *Wisdom Sits in Places: Landscape and Language Among the Western Apache*. (Albuquerque, NM: University of New Mexico Press, 1996).
Bauman, Zygmunt. *Consuming Life*. (Malden, MA: Polity, 2007).
Bauman, Zygmunt. *Does Ethics Stand a Chance in a World of Consumers?* (Cambridge: Harvard University Press, 2008).
Bauman, Zygmunt. *Liquid Modernity*. (New York: Polity, 2000).
Bauman, Zygmunt. *Modernity and Ambivalence*. (Ithaca, NY: Cornell University Press, 1991).
Bauman, Zygmunt. *Postmodern Ethics* (Malden: Blackwell Publishing, 1990).
Bauman, Zygmunt . *The Individualized Society*. (Malden, MA: Polity, 2001).
Bauman, Zygmunt. *Thinking Sociologically* (Cambridge: Blackwell Publishers, 1990).
Berg, Maggie and Barabara K. Seeber. *The Slow Professor: Challenging the Culture of Speed in the Academy*. (Toronto, CA: The University of Toronto Press, 2016).
Blair, Ann M., *Too Much to Know: Managing Scholarly Information before the Modern Age*. (New Haven, CT: Yale University Press, 2011).
Bledstein, Burton J. *The Culture of Professionalism: The Middle Class and the Development of Higher Education in America*. (New York: Norton, 1978).
Boldeman, Lee. *The Cult of the Market: Economic Fundamentalism and its Discontents*. (Canberra, Australia, ANU E Press, 2011).

Caputo, John D. *What Would Jesus Deconstruct: The Good News of Postmodernism for the Church*. (Ada, MI: Baker Press, 2007).

Carson, Rabecca, Et Al. *Politics of the Many: Contemporary Radical Thought and the Crisis of Agency*. (NY: Bloomsbury Publishing, 2021).

Clark, Christopher. *The Roots of Rural Capitalism: Western Massachusetts 1780 – 1860*. (Ithica, NY: Cornell University Press, 1992).

Clark, William. *Academic Charisma and the Origins of the Research University*. (Chicago, IL: University of Chicago Press, 2006).

Cox, Harvey. *The Market as God*. (Cambridge, MA: Harvard University Press, 2016).

Deleuze, Gilles. "Postscript on the Societies of Control." *October*, vol. 59, 1992.

Deloria, Jr., Vine. *Spirit and Reason: The Vine Deloria, Jr., Reader*. (Golden, CO: Fulcrum, 1999).

Descartes, Rene. *Meditations on First Philosophy* (Cambridge, UK: Cambridge University Press, 1996).

Ewen Stewart. *Captains of Consciousness: Advertising and the Social Roots of the Consumer Culture*. (New York, NY: Basic Books, 2001).

Federici, Silvia. *Caliban and the Witch: Women, the Body and Primitive Accumulation*. (NY: Autonomedia, 2004).

Fraser, Nancy. *Cannibal Capitalism: How Our System is Devouring Democracy, Care and the Planet—and What We Can Do about It*. (NY: Verso, 2022).

Fraser, Nancy. "Feminism, Capitalism, and the Cunning of History". *New Left Review* 56: Mar/Apr 2009.

Fraser, Nancy. *Fortunes of Feminism: From State-Managed Capitalism to Neoliberal Crisis*. (Brooklyn, NY: Verso, 2013).

Foucault, Michel. *Discipline and Punish*. (New York: NY: Vintage Books, 1995).

Foucault, Michel . *Power/Knowledge*. (New York: Vintage, 1980).

Foucault, Michel. *The History of Sexuality, Volume 1*. (New York: NY: Vintage Books, 1990).

Giddens, Anthony. *The Consequences of Modernity*. (Stanford: Stanford University Press, 1991).

Graeber, David. *Debt: The First 5,000 Years*. (Brooklyn, NY: Melville House, 2014).

Graeber, David and David Wengrow, *The Dawn of Everything: A New History of Humanity*. (NY: Farrar, Straus and Giroux, 2021).

Green, Anna and Kathleen Troup. *The Houses of History: A Critical Reader in Twentieth-Century History and Theory*. (New York, NY : NYU Press, 1999).

Han, Byung-Chul. *Capitalism and the Death Drive*. (Cambridge, UK: Polity Press, 2022).

Han, Byung-Chul. *The Burnout Society*. (Cambridge, UK: Polity Press, 2010).

Han, Byung-Chul. *The Crisis of Narration*. (Cambridge, UK: Polity Press, 2024).

Hardt Michael and Antonio Negri. Empire. (Cambridge, MA: Harvard University Press, 2001).

Heidegger, Martin: "Memorial Address." *Discourse on Thinking*. (NY: Harper & Row, 1966).

Hénaff, Marcel. *The Price of Truth: Gift, Money and Philosophy*. (Stanford: Stanford University Press, 2010).

Hirshman, Albert. *The Passions and the Interests: Political Arguments for Capitalism before Its Triumph*. (Princeton, NJ: Princeton University Press, 1977).

Hobsbawm, Eric, *The Age of Capital:1848-1875* (New York, NY: Vintage, 1996).

Hochschild, Arlie Russel. *The Commercialization of Intimate Life: Notes from Home and Work*. (Berkeley, CA: University of California Press, 2003).

Jonas, Hans. *The Imperative of Responsibility: In Search of an Ethics of a Technological Age* (Chicago: University of Chicago Press, 1985).

Kuhn, Thomas. *The Structure of Scientific Revolutions*. (Chicago: University of Chicago Press, 1996).

Levinas, Emmanuel. *Totality and Infinity*. (Pittsburg, PA: Duquesne University Press, 2003).

Marcuse, Herbert. *One Dimensional Man: Studies in the Ideology of Advanced Industrial Society*. (Boston, MA: Beacon Press, 1991).

McCarraher, Eugene. *The Enchantments of Mammon: How Capitalism became the Religion of Modernity*.

Menand, Louis. *The Metaphysical Club: A Story of Ideas in America*. (New York, NY: Farrar, Straus and Giroux, 2002).

Merchant, Carolyn. *The Death of Nature: Women Ecology and the Scientific Revolution*. (New York: Harper and Row, 1990).

Mies, Maria. *Patriarchy and Accumulation On A World Scale: Women in the International Division of Labour*. (London, UK: Zed Books, 1999).

Mills, Charles W. *The Racial Contract*. Ithaca, NY: Cornell University Press, 1997).

Nietzsche, Friedrich, *Beyond Good and Evil: Prelude to a Philosophy of the Future* (New York, NY: Vintage, 1989),

Nietzsche, Friedrich, *On the Future of Our Educational Institutions. The Complete Works of Friedrich Nietzsche, Vol 3*. (Edinburgh, Eng: Morrison and Gibb Limited, 1910).

Nietzsche, Friedrich, *The Birth of Tragedy* (New York, NY: Dover, 1995).

Nietzsche, Friedrich, *The Gay Science* (New York, NY: Vintage, 1974).

Nietzsche, Friedrich, *The Genealogy of Morals* (New York, NY: Oxford University Press, 1999).

Nietzsche, Friedrich, *The Portable Nietzsche* (New York, New York: Penguin Books, 1977).

Nietzsche, Friedrich, *The Will to Power* (New York, NY: Vintage, 1968).
Ortega y Gasset, José. *History as a System and Other Essays Toward a Philosophy of History.* (New York: Norton and Company, 1961).
Ortega y Gasset, José. *Man and Crisis.* (New York: Norton and Company, 1958).
Ortega y Gasset, José. *Meditations on Quixote.* (New York: Norton and Company, 1963).
Ortega y Gasset, José. *The Mission of the Librarian.* (Boston, MA: G.K. Hall, 1961).
Ortega y Gasset, José. *The Mission of the University.* (New York: Norton and Company, 1944).
Ortega y Gasset, José. *The Revolt of the Masses.* (New York: Norton and Company, 1991).
Ortega y Gasset, José. *What is Philosophy?* (New York: Norton and Company, 1964).
Pack, Justin. *Amor Mundi and Overcoming Modern World Alienation.* (NY: Lexington Press, 2019).
Pack, Justin. *How the Neoliberalization of Academia Leads to Thoughtlessness: Arendt and the Modern University.* (New York: Lexington Books, 2018).
Pack, Justin. "Is it Morally Wrong to Publish?" in *Philosophical Interventions in Neoliberal Higher Education.* (Lexington Press, forthcoming).
Pack, Justin. *Meritocracy Mingled with Scripture.* (By Common Consent Press, 2024).
Pack, Justin. *Money and Thoughtlessness: A Genealogy and Defense of Traditions Suspicions of Money and Merchants.*(NY: Palgrave Macmillan, 2023).
Pack, Justin. *Prehistoric Philosophy: The Neolithic Revolution, the Indigenous Critique, and the Myths of Civilization.* (Bloomsbury Press, forthcoming).
Pack, Justin. "The Need for an Ethics of Sustainable Knowledge Production." *Metaphilosophy* vol. 50, no. 4. July, 2019.
Pateman, Carole. *The Sexual Contract.* (NY: Polity Press, 1988).
Patterson, Orlando. *Slavery and Social Death.* (Cambridge: Harvard University Press, 2018).
Polanyi, Karl. *The Great Transformation: The Political and Economic Origins of Our Time.* (Boston, MA: Beacon Press, 2001).
Rorty, Richard. *Philosophy and the Mirror of Nature.* (Princeton: Princeton University Press, 1981).
Rudolph, Frederick. *The American College and University: A History.* (Athens, GA: University of Georgia, 1990).
Sahlins, Marshall. *Stone Age Economics.* (Chicago: Aldine, 1994).
Sandel, Michael. *What Money Can't Buy: The Moral Limits of Markets.* (NY: Farrar, Straus and Giroux, 2013).

Schmidt, Dennis J. *On Germans and Other Greeks* (Bloomington, IN: Indiana University Press, 2001.

Scott, James C. *Seeing Like A State: How Certain Schemes to Improve the Human Condition Have Failed*. (New Haven, CN: Yale University Press, 1998).

Strasser, Suan, *Satisfaction Guaranteed: The Making of the American Mass Market*. (Washington DC: Smithsonian Books, 2004).

Stern, Fritz. *The Varieties of History from Voltaire to the Present*. (New York, NY: Vintage Books, 1973).

Taylor, Charles. *A Secular Age*. (Cambridge, MA: Harvard University Press, 2007).

Taylor, Charles. *Sources of the Self: The Making of Modern Identity*. (Boston, MA: Harvard University Press, 1992).

Tucker, ed., *The Marx and Engels Reader (Second Edition)*. (New York: W.W. Norton & Company, 1978).

Weber, Eugen. Peasants Into Frenchmen: The Modernization of Rural France, 1870 – 1914. (CA: Stanford University Press, 1976).

Weber. Max. *The Protestant Ethic and the Spirit of Capitalism*. (New York, NY: Routledge, 2002).

Young, Julian. *Friedrich Nietzsche: A Philosophical Biography* (New York, NY: Cambridge University Press, 2010).

Young, Julian, ed. *Individual and Community in Nietzsche's Philosophy*. (NY: Cambridge University Press, 2012).

Young, Julian. *Nietzsche's Philosophy of Religion* (New York, NY: Cambridge University Press, 2006).

Young, Julian. *The Death of God and the Meaning of Life*. (New York: Routledge, 2014).

INDEX

academic production   119–26, 189
academic publishing   164–74
accumulation   5–6, 9, 29, 117–19
Arendt, Hannah
   action, work and labor   76–8
   Amor Mundi   69–74
   earth   69–71
   modern world alienation   74–8
   the new   83–5
   nihilism   78–83
   science   75–6
   world   69–74, 78–85

Bauman, Zygmunt   4, 6–7, 122–5, 132–4
   on liquid modernity   134–40

cacophony   1–9, 15–16, 177–90
capitalism   1–2, 5, 95–100
centripetal *vs.* centrifugal work   184–8
consumption   126–30
counterhegemony   1, 11

dual structure of cacophonous capitalism   108–11, 138–9

environmental crisis   1–4, 91–2, 184, 189
Eriksen, Thomas Hylland   3, 148–56

Federici, Silvia   105–6
feminism   10

Fraser, Nancy   1–2, 10, 133–4, 185–6
freedom   7, 77–8
Future Shock   89–90

Han, Byung-Chul   156–63
Homo economicus   7, 32–3, 63, 91, 100–3

Jonas, Hans   4

Kierkegaard, Soren   179

meritocracy   103–5
money   95–108
myth   19–21, 23–4, 27–35, 95–100

Nietzsche
   affirmation of life   21–4
   amor fati and Eternal Recurrence   64–8
   community   17, 23–4
   descartes   25–6
   dual structure of nihilism   31–3
   instincts   17–21, 24–8, 32–3
   modern cacophony   24–31
   myth   19–21, 23–4, 27–35
   nihilism   31–3, 78
   nihilistic abundance   8–9, 30
   romantic conservative   16–9
   science   67–8
   self   25–7
   socrates   25–9

Nihilism 7-9, 31-3
Nova effect 5, 63, 92-5

Ortega y Gasset
   culture 54-6
   democracy 47-50, 58
   increase of life 45-7
   instincts 44-5
   integration 53-6
   noble life and barbarism 47-50
   science 50-3, 56

selva selvaggia 42-5
specialization 50-3

production 117-19

radical movements 1

Taylor, Charles 4, 93
too much 9, 15, 33
transgression 9-10, 130-4, 138-42

Young, Julian 17-20 34-5